1960

# CATHERINE OF SIENA

# IV. THE REFORMATION

# V. THE PASSION

# VI. DEATH

# I. The Beginnings

# 1. Catherine Discovers God

Lapa, daughter of Muccio (or Puccio) Placenti, when she became the bride of the dyer,[1] Giacomo Benincasa, brought him little by way of dowry. Like him, she came from a family of Sienese artisans. She brought him, as recompense for her small dowry, untiring devotion to duty, an energetic character, and a fruitful maternity.

In Siena they lived in the populous and noisy district of the painters, called the Fondebranda quarter, where their home, with its workshop and office, was set down in a crowded group of habitations among steep, narrow streets. There Giacomo worked, mostly in silence, while Lapa did the talking and directed that caravan of children who came along, one after another, governing the complex business of an industrious house in an epoch of crisis in which the rulers of the city were torn by factions, military campaigns were waged by mercenary troops, and the population was periodically decimated by plague.

The Middle Ages were coming to a close and the Modern Age was emerging; political, economic, and social transformations were taking place, to the accompaniment of bitter struggles, violent hatreds, plots, desolation, and ruin — whose results were keenly felt by the modest dyer, even as he took his part in them. Through these very dissensions the artisan classes were slowly but surely destroying the powers of the noble families, who had been exercising their nobility principally by clearing the lists of the bourgeoisie and tearing each other to pieces, thus literally vying with each other in preparing the way for the tyranny of a war lord — native or foreign — who would be capable of bringing order out of the licentiousness which was strangling men's liberties.

Along with the fruits of his home-conducted business, Giacomo passed on to his children the virtues of a righteous man, measured in his speech and with his conscience clear; Lapa instilled in them a spirit of exertion and of hard work and, despite her wagging tongue, communicated to them the simple rectitude of a God-fearing woman. Likewise, daughter, as she was, of a poet-artisan, she put into their education a quality of belligerent beauty.

The biographer of St. Catherine, Blessed Raymond of Capua, of the Pier delle Vigne family, theologian and Master General of the Dominicans, who had known Lapa well, calls her a "fruitful bee" who "filled the house of Giacomo with sons and daughters." Indeed, she bore twenty-five children. Among the boys there was an Alexander, a Bartolo, a Stephen and, among the girls, a Nicolucci, a Bonaventura, a Giovanna, a Lisa, a Nera, and Catherine — her twenty-fourth.

Catherine was born, along with her twin sister, Giovanna, March 25, 1347, the Feast of the Annunciation of the Blessed Virgin, which that year fell on Palm Sunday. Giovanna died at birth; Catherine was nursed by her mother, who up to this time had — because of successive pregnancies — turned over her babies to nurses.

The last child was born in the terrible plague of 1348, described by Boccaccio, in which in Siena alone more than 30,000 citizens perished. It was the Black Death which, ravaging all Europe, not only depopulated whole regions but also brought about a momentous change in the thinking of men, so that from its black womb came forth the modern age, with its revolt against the Pope and its start on the way to humanism.

Of her twenty-four brothers and sisters only some names are

known to us and these in relation to Catherine, who was evidently an extraordinary creature, considering that she rose from the crushing mediocrity of economic distress, from illnesses and all sorts of destitution to become one of the most potent and original personalities to be found in all history. We know that as a child she was charming, lively, highly intelligent. Her shining eyes, pensive but quick, missed nothing. Her young mind, eager to grasp ideas, rose to things divine, especially when, at evening time, around a blazing fire, in the midst of her family Catherine listened to readings from the *Leggenda Aurea*, written by the saintly Bishop of Genoa, Jacopo da Varagine, which brought to life for humble folk the figures of the saints. Jacopo da Varagine had been one of those Dominicans — and they were rather numerous — who had worked to popularize the writings of the Fathers of the Church, thus to make better known the truths of religion: Domenico Cavalca, for example, who had written *Lives of the Holy Fathers of Thebes*; Jacopo Pasavanti, author of the *Mirror of True Penance*; Bartolomeo di San Concordio, Giordano da Tivalto, and others. The child's fancy was quickly aroused by romantic adventures, by the careers of the hermits. From those pages she learned how the servants of God modeled themselves upon Jesus in prodigies of mortification and love; and Catherine eagerly absorbed all the accounts, falling hopelessly in love with that Jesus who inspired such heroes, and convincing herself how urgent it was for her, too, to dedicate herself in heroic measure to the will of God.

Among the stories read to her, one that particularly struck her was the romantic adventure of a noble young woman of Alexandria who secretly consecrated herself to God and then, so as not to be compelled by her parents to marry a wealthy young man of the city, dressed herself in men's clothing, fled from her home, and masquerading as a man was admitted to a monastery and lived for years as a monk. Catherine was so impressed by this extraordinary adventure that she planned to do the same thing. She carried out her plan to the extent of deciding to adopt her heroine's name, a name that sounded a bit like her own, but also expressed the notion of joy, and of God's freedom — Eufrosina (Gr. *euphrosyne* —

cheerfulness, delight). There sprang full blown from her heart a galaxy of supernatural figures: above them all hovered Jesus and Mary, and SS. Dominic, Paul, and Euphrosina. From them came such interior joy, such continuous stream of inspiration, that those around her were charmed.

Thus in Catherine's religious experience occurred at the outset what in the greatest saints has occurred, as a rule, only after great trials and years of self-discipline: her heart was filled with the presence of God and of the supernatural. She was like an angel on earth, able to impart to others that which was locked up in her own heart: God. It is hardly to be marveled at, then, that when she was but six years old she received her first sensible vision of another world.

Returning one day with her little brother, Stephen, from a visit to their married sister, Bonaventura, while crossing the street called Valle Piatta (now known as Cotone), she raised her eyes between the high enclosing walls and saw above the Church of St. Dominic the radiant and imposing figure of Christ the King, crowned with a miter, attired in a gorgeous robe, and seated upon a throne, flanked by the Apostles Peter, Paul, and John. She poured out her soul in adoration to the Lord of the universe, who smiled at her and raised His hand in benediction. Catherine was rooted to the spot in contemplation. Peasants and beasts of burden passed by unnoticed; while her little brother, thinking she was right behind him, went on home. When he realized that she was not with him, he went back and called to her, but she did not hear. Her eyes were fixed upon the thrilling vision above the roofs. Stephen rushed up and shook her, calling, "Catherine! Catherine! What's the matter? Why don't you come home?" Catherine turned, reluctantly, as if awakening from a dream. "If you could see what I see, not for all the gold in the world would you have torn me from that lovely vision." Then she turned back to look at the heavenly throne. But it was no longer there, and she began to weep softly for having turned her glance away from her Lord.

Catherine's vocation was now determined. God had blessed her for all eternity: she belonged to Him forever. She knew now that her existence must be consumed in glorifying the King of kings, to be one day by the side of the Apostles, she, an insignificant little creature, the daughter of a dyer, from the poorest part of town.

The Pope who canonized St. Catherine, the learned Pius II, would declare that her wisdom was not acquired but infused, that is to say, received directly from God, inspired. And we can well believe that from her earliest years she knew in the same way of the sanctity of Christian heroes, among them her beloved Fathers of the desert — by inspiration rather than by reading.

Catherine was physically vigorous. However, from the time she saw the vision, she embarked upon the road to sanctity with a determination that showed her stamina of character, imitating those heroes also in her penances, convinced that by overcoming the flesh she could make her existence a thing wholly spiritual. So as a child, instead of taking part in games, she would draw apart to pray, to meditate and, when she could, to scourge with a sharp cord the body to which she was already denying necessary food. Indeed, already brought to the point of heroism, of totally dedicating herself, as young as she was she conceived the idea of imitating the Fathers of the desert, by withdrawing to a hermitage. Consequently one day, providing herself with a loaf of bread, she set out toward the gate of St. Ansano, in the vicinity of which her married sister lived, and passing out beyond the city walls by a steep path she started across the fields. It seemed to her that she was already in the desert: the neighborhood was unknown, mysterious, and awe-inspiring. She found a cave and entered it. Now a life of holiness, of anchorite ascent to God, was opened to her too! She began to pray with such rapture that her body was raised from the ground and remained so until about three o'clock that afternoon.

Down to earth again, however, she understood from God that life in the desert was not for her. Becoming perhaps a bit frightened, she decided to return to her family, for whom the whole episode had passed unnoticed, for they thought that she had been visiting her sister.

This feeling for asceticism, with its turning of thoughts toward God, lent Catherine an attraction for the other little girls around her — who listened to her and tried to imitate her. She taught them how to pray, and imposed upon them fast and penances, binding them to herself not by frivolous tricks but by the love of God.

Nevertheless Catherine, though always thoughtful, meditative, and recollected, remained always happy and obliging: her interior life kept her always in contact with the source of joy, God Himself, and united with Him she showed forth, as water from a spring bubbles up toward the sun, the perfect joy promised by Christ.

She liked to run up the stairs of her home four at a time, so that she seemed to be flying. However, so as not to frighten her mother, she often made herself walk up, reciting a *Hail Mary* at each step. All her sprightliness seemed her way of hastening her return to the house of her Father, where Mary and the saints awaited her. Her growth in years, her becoming of age, were in her mind an avid approach to the true life.

These childish attitudes of Catherine are significant: all her life she remained a child — open, ingenuous, and spontaneous to the action of divine grace. Later on when she took part in critical world events, and knew men and women in every state of life, in her inmost soul she preserved the wisdom of a child and remained always a trusting little girl in the hands of her Father.

From 1354 onward Catherine's life clearly followed the promises of the vision: she moved directly toward God, striving ever to glorify His name. And to dedicate herself entirely to this task, in imitation of Euphrosina and, still more, of the Virgin Mary, she was convinced that she should consecrate herself to Jesus by a vow of virginity. Child of a family in which there was always talk of marriage as a means of security and of increasing patrimony, she understood that a girl was early destined to have a husband and to orientate her life toward him. But for her, as for numerous other virgins honored by the Church, there could be no other spouse than Jesus. Once having understood this, she directed all her affection to Him, with an application that would admit no wavering.

So at the age of seven she made a vow of virginity. She made it one day withdrawn to a remote corner of the house where no one could hear her. Kneeling in the silence, she pronounced a formula of consecration to the Virgin, a formula which she herself was later to repeat on more than one occasion to her confessor, Father Raymond, and to those closest to her:

"O most blessed and most holy Virgin, who, first among all women, consecrated thy virginity to the Lord, whence thou became by His grace, mother of His only-begotten Son, I pray thy ineffable mercy not to regard my merits nor my littleness, but deign to grant me the great grace of giving me as my Spouse Him whom I desire with all the powers of my soul, thy most Holy Son, the one Lord Jesus Christ; and I promise Him and Thee not to have any other spouse and to do all I can to preserve intact my purity."

It may well be that the expressions used by the little girl in formulating her vow were more simple than this and that this rather elaborate form is the work of the theologian, her confessor, who put into Latin a confession made to him by Catherine years after the event; however, this was its substance. Little Catherine already knew the manner of saints in this regard — and these ambitious words were not beyond her childish understanding. Indeed her sentiments could hardly be contained even in the formula given: she spoke with a soul enamored and entirely dedicated. She was of the same stuff as other resolute and serene virgins: Mary, Agnes, Lucy, and Clara among them.

Detached from the world she began now to develop a religious vocation that was to lead her to a religious order. She turned her attention from the individualism of the desert Fathers to Fathers of the newly formed Order of Preachers, the Dominicans. For in her vision had she not seen the throne of the Most High over the church of St. Dominic? It symbolized for her the truth, the light of wisdom, that spirituality which combined human reason and divine, corresponding so well with her own spirit, eager for light. In her thoughts she conceived such veneration for those religious that when one of them passed her home she noted the cobblestones touched by his feet and then secretly followed to kiss them. As has been said she dreamed of one day, like Euphrosina, dressing as a man and going off to find admission in a Dominican Friary. In this childish aspiration we find a trace of that virility, complementing her zest for reason, her desire for wisdom, which was later to reveal itself as a typical characteristic of her personality.

NOTE: Chapter 1

1. *tintore*. Sig. Giordani states Benincasa's occupation simply as "dyer"; the new *Encyclopedia Catholic* (Vol. III, p. 1151) gives it as *tintore di pelli*; i.e., dyer of skins, leather.

## 2. She Defends Her Virginity

As if to confirm Catherine's growing-up — spiritually and physically — a curious episode occurred about this time.

One day her mother sent her off to the parish church of St. Anthony to ask the curate to offer a Mass in honor of the Saint. Catherine took candles and coins to place as an offering upon the altar, and went off on her errand. It so happened that as she entered the church a priest was just coming from the sacristy to celebrate Mass and the girl decided to stay for it. Lapa, who had intended that her daughter should leave the Mass offering and come right back home, was displeased at Catherine's delay and greeted her with a torrential outburst. The scolding, from the heart of an overworked housewife, ended: "And a curse on the evil tongues that said you would not come back at all!"

It was perhaps too crude an attempt to punish the girl, who was really incapable of deliberately displeasing her mother. Catherine stood in silence, grieving; then, drawing her mother aside, she gave her, with all due respect, a little lecture, which we may thus summarize: "Mother dear, when I fail to obey you, punish me as you think right and proper, so that on another occasion I shall be

11

more obedient, as I should be. But in heaven's name, don't give your tongue to cursing your neighbor, good or evil though she be, because at your age this is not good and it makes me suffer." Lapa was petrified. The remarks of this young daughter, so well beloved, were so far beyond her years, yet so respectfully uttered, that the loquaciousness left Lapa speechless. When she found her voice, she demanded: "Why were you so long away?" "Because I assisted at the Mass you wanted to have celebrated; just as soon as it was over I came straight home."

The mother meditated at length upon these observations of the child whose behavior astounded her more and more from day to day. And when Giacomo returned from his shop she told him the whole story; and that good man, too, asked himself what would become of that daughter of theirs, who was so precocious.

Lapa had by now realized that Catherine's spirit was leading her apart. She sensed that the child held aloof; and since she was a woman of authority and tenaciousness, she wanted to recall her little sheep to the customary paths of people the world over: the people who, little by little, by their labors, through their marriage, by working together, deliberately achieve positions in the world economically and socially more advantageous. So, as the child grew into adolescence, the mother sought to restrain her, to control her. Catherine was pretty and vivacious: she should become an envied wife, a prosperous mother. Hence, from the time that Catherine was twelve years old, her mother kept her at home, according to the fashion of that day. From her twelfth birthday a girl was prepared for marriage, and it was not considered proper that she should go out to show herself but rather that she should await her suitors at her home, engaged in domestic affairs, under the watchful eyes of her parents. Lapa and Giacomo Benincasa, seeing that Catherine grew up serious and virtuous, set about to find her a good match. With this in mind, Lapa began to speak to her daughter about such a future and to urge her to dress up a bit, to emphasize her good points and show forth her natural attractiveness.

A hidden conflict between Catherine and her family began. She was espoused to God, and they wanted to espouse her to a man.

To devote herself entirely to her Spouse and bring to Him the dowry of all her virtues, Catherine divested herself of all worldly ornamentation and subjected her body to penances; the family, who knew nothing of the interior life of the girl, wanted to educate her in worldly ways, to deck her out in fine dresses, and make-up. But the mother, despite all argument, could not interest her daughter in marriage. So Lapa turned for help to her married daughter, Bonaventura, whom Catherine loved greatly. And indeed, to satisfy her sister, Catherine actually agreed to dress up a bit, but with no practical result; for she never showed herself outside the house in her fine clothes. Yet, even though she had dressed up only to satisfy her sister — an act of charity, surely, toward one she loved and in no sense a renunciation of home and her dream — Catherine wept about it for the rest of her life as if she had sinned. Characteristically she felt that her own faults were the cause of evil to everybody around her.

As a matter of fact every time that she wore some trinket or arranged her hair with care, she intensified her penances afterward, occupying her free time in prayer and meditation. She denied herself sleep and food — never tasting meat at all.

As if to put an end to the torment that it was for her to devote even a little attention to her personal appearance, Bonaventura died suddenly. The instigating ceased.

Out of this whole experience there remained in Catherine's heart a bitter taste whence came a complete disesteem of herself, along with her holy fear of God. She was convinced that she was a sinner; she likened herself to Mary Magdalene, seeing in that penitent woman an example of her own conduct. Certainly, however, in Catherine's case those actions had not been sinful: we have strong declarations to this effect from eminent theologians, including Catherine's confessor. At most, she had been guilty of overindulging the wishes of her sister; or, as it seems to this writer, Catherine's experience was permitted by God to cleanse, of the most subtle tarnishes, a soul destined to make known again the face of Christ in a society disorientated and troubled which, amid the destructions of wars and plagues and violent partisanships, in the midst of radical economic and social transformations, was moving toward skepticism and materialism and about to give birth to humanism.

This providence of God served to increase Catherine's distrust of herself and to lead her along the path of humility, where the soul neither sees nor hears anything but God. At this time Catherine made a prime discovery about herself: she received the first glimmerings of what she was later to call the "knowledge of herself," in which she found a place of refuge, a cloister, an interior solitude.

The destruction of self-love, within this interior solitude, was integrated by an ever increasing warfare upon her body, to overcome sensual impulses, and by an intensified search for suffering, so that she made her own even the sufferings of those around her, in order to have a "part in the sufferings of Him, a conformity with His death," as the Apostle Paul had written — that "Little Paul" whom Catherine so much meditated upon and loved, from whom she was learning how to be united to her Spouse. For it was he who had pointed to "those whom He has foreknown (and) whom He has also predestined to become conformed to the image of His Son" (Rom. 8:29). Such predestination was Catherine's. So it was that with her absorption in meditations and penances, her determined detachment from the world, more and more she shunned the company of outsiders, and especially of men. She lived at home as in a hermitage in the desert, almost as an exile. Her heart rose far above the routine of family affairs and plans for her to found a new household, and she grieved her parents, keen as they were to marry off this other daughter and to procure for her an advantageous family name, especially now that Bonaventura was dead.

Then Lapa got the idea to have recourse to an influential Dominican friar, a Father Tommaso della Fonte who, in addition to being a son of St. Dominic was related to the Benincasa family. He was the brother-in-law of a sister of Catherine's. He had been orphaned at the age of ten, when his mother, Nicoluccia, died during the plague of 1348, and he had been received into the home of Giacomo. He had been among those who, around the family hearth on long winter evenings, had read aloud to attentive listeners the Lives of the Saints taken from the *Leggenda Aurea* and other volumes probably borrowed from the Dominican convent of Camporeggi. When he became a Dominican himself he was distinguished by rare prudence and lively charity so that he became the spiritual director and follower of the virgin of Siena.

To satisfy the parents, Fra Tommaso, who had known the girl since she was a baby, had a conference with her and questioned her. Catherine confided in him her desire to live outside of marriage, to dedicate herself to the Lord. The friar understood; and he advised her, not as a human relative, but as a spiritual kinsman: "The moment that you are absolutely sure you want to serve the Lord exclusively and your parents urge you to do otherwise, show them how steadfast is your determination by cutting off your hair. Then, perhaps, they will quiet down."

A bold stroke: the shears would cut her off from the world. There was in the fearless and tranquil suggestion of the friar the straightforwardness of Christ's own call: Come follow Me . . . he who will not leave father and mother. . . . It had been thus that Francis had dealt with Clara: he cut off that marvelous head of hair and in a twinkling he had taken her from the world.

But Catherine took shears herself and cut off her abundant hair; then she covered her head with a cap and from that day forward wore a veil. She was then fifteen years old.

Lapa was, of course, amazed at this new costume and demanded to know what it meant. When the daughter replied evasively Lapa angrily tore off the veil. The loss of that hair which had been a matter of family pride seemed to the mother like the ruin of a castle. At Lapa's cries, Catherine's father and brothers came running in. They, too, felt that her gesture seemed to have been made in contempt of them, to set at naught all their plans. They determined to force her to do their will. To begin with they took away from her the room into which she could retire to meditate and pray, and they made her sleep with a brother and sister. Next they made her work in the kitchen as a substitute for the servant. Thus occupied all day with taking care of a large house and numerous family she would have no time to indulge her caprices. They treated her like a servant; they made her a drudge; they called her bad names; she was a living ignominy to her family. They thought abuse would succeed where persuasion had failed.

But though Catherine was without a room with four walls, she had an inner cell from which no violence could expel her. Though her family treated her as a servant, she was happy to serve them, raising their persons to a supernatural plane where she saw Jesus in her father, Mary in her mother, and the Apostles in her brothers, and in that light, kitchen and cellar and bedroom were transfigured into a temple — a sort of Paradise — and every act, even washing dishes and sweeping floors became an act of religion.

Compelled to share a room with one of her brothers, Catherine chose the room of Stephen. He was unmarried and also he had been her companion on that evening, long ago, when Christ the King had appeared to her; and therefore with him, Catherine felt less hindered. In that room, then, by day when her brother was away at work, Catherine had privacy for prayer, and when he slept at night she crouched upon her bed to pray in the darkness. In keeping her in the house for the most difficult chores her parents, unwittingly, helped her to live more removed from the world, as she desired.

In the long hours of work and recollection, Catherine's vocation took definite form. She meditated upon the religious orders, trying to decide in which one she could best dedicate herself in sacred virginity. Her decision was that the Dominican order would conform to her aspirations. The ardor for truth, the linear logic, the fighting spirit with which St. Dominic and St. Peter the Martyr had become such valiant champions against error, the hunger for intellectual speculation in the ministry of God of which St. Thomas Aquinas had been a daring pioneer, all fired the flame of her love, which in her was one with truth. Consecrate them to the service of truth, our Lord had prayed at the Last Supper; and Catherine wanted to consecrate herself to truth, for she loved God as *Truth*. The desire to don the white and black of the Order of Penance, in which already so many women had sought to become saints, burned within her to the point that the holy Father Dominic appeared to her in a vision, extended to her a white habit, and assured her that despite all opposition she would wear it. Comforted by the vision, she took the first opportunity she could find to talk to her family together — probably at the evening *veglia*[1] in the ample kitchen after she had served them at supper — and she came right to the point, sure of herself. She told them that she had kept silent until now out of the reverence that by God's command she owed her parents. But that time for silence had passed. She told them how, as a little girl, after mature reflection, she had made a vow of virginity to Jesus and Mary; and how her determination had grown so much stronger with the years that any attempt to thwart it was doomed to failure. So the family might as well stop insisting that she marry: she was going to obey God rather than men. They could lock her in the house; they could throw her into the street as a vagabond; but her heart would not change. Espoused to the Omnipotent, she did not fear the test; in any eventuality He would take care of her.

Her discourse, spoken with such conviction and modesty, inspired by all the sincerity of her soul, impressed her listeners around the table: more than one of them burst into tears. They were sons of Siena, a city that was quarrelsome yet religious, which after the victory of Montaperti[2] had gained the name *civitas Virginis* — the city of the Virgin — and looking at Catherine they seemed to see Mary. There followed an emotion-packed pause. In the father's mind there passed in review the many extraordinary actions of his daughter. He recalled, for one thing, the day he had surprised her in Stephen's room and had seen that while she prayed, as if raised in ecstasy, a dove fluttered above her head. It was as though he were just then really discovering in his daughter, flesh of his flesh, his better self, the secret of his own religious preoccupations. He rose to speak, uniting all the Christian wisdom of the artisan with the paternal love which never failed him: "God forbid, my dear daughter," he said, drying his tears, "that we should in any way contradict the divine Will, from which, as we all realize, comes your holy intention. At last we are certain that you are not moved by the caprice of youth, but by an impulse of divine love. Fulfill your vow, then, by holy plans and we shall not interfere. Pray for us, so that we may be worthy of the promise of your Betrothed, Whom, by His grace, you chose in your earliest years."

There was silence among the family, male and female, married and single, bound together by the love of God and by the wisdom of Giacomo. He was mild-mannered, but he was the head of the family; then he continued to his astonished family: "From now on let no one annoy this dearest daughter of mine. Let no one dare in any way to interfere with her. Let her serve her Spouse as she wishes, and may she pray for us without ceasing. We could never dare hope for a relationship such as this; we must not lament in the least when instead of a mortal man we receive into our midst a God and a Man immortal."

Listening to their father, they understood the daughter better. And he, without knowing it, was becoming a disciple of Catherine; just as Lapa would become in later years. Now, chastened and resigned, she restored Catherine's own room to her. Lapa was not the type to admit defeat; but here was the matter of God's will, and besides that here was Giacomo's will — Giacomo a man of God whom the entire family looked upon as venerable in the sight of the Lord.

NOTES:  Chapter 2

1. The family reunion, especially among peasants, to pass time in the evening after supper.
2. The bloody battle of Montaperti, near Siena, in 1260, in which the Florentine Guelfs were utterly put to rout by the Sienese and the Florentine Ghibellines under the leadership of Farinata. Cf. Dante, Purgatorio, X 85–88; XXXII, 79–81.

# 3. Sister of Penance

Free now to live as God inspired her, Catherine devoted herself to her own sanctification along the lines already laid out: charity, recollections, penance. Penance to overcome the flesh and to plunge the entire person into spiritual life, to unite her to God and to begin in time the life of eternity. She had again a little room of her own; she chose the narrowest and most inconvenient one. It was above the kitchen, with a little window looking over the narrow street of the Tiratoio.[1] She furnished it to her own taste: a bench, upon which in the daytime she and her visitors could be seated and which served at night as her bed; and a chest to keep her clothes. She hung a crucifix on the wall and set a small lamp to burn beneath it. In the chest she kept — along with her small supply of linen — her instruments of penance: sackcloth, chains, scourges.

It is said that her every flagellation — and at that time she scourged herself three times a day in imitation of St. Dominic — lasted about an hour and a half. Always present in her mind was Jesus, scourged and bleeding, who for love of us shed the blood of our redemption, and she wanted to imitate Him. Summer and winter, day and night, she wore wool. She slept only half an hour every other day.

She ate no meat, drank no wine. Her food consisted of a few vegetables.

Lapa shed tears at such desolation; and some nights, when she could contain herself no longer, she would take her extraordinary and incomprehensible daughter into her own bedroom, and make her lie down beside her; only to discover, upon waking, that Catherine had slipped away. The poor mother was distracted; and one day when she surprised her daughter, covered with blood from head to foot in the midst of a scourging, she screamed: "My daughter, my daughter, you are killing yourself! Who has taken my daughter from me?" And tearing her hair, she started running through the house screaming as if mortally wounded, so that the neighbors came rushing in.

In the eyes of Lapa, who loved God, yes, but in a measured way that took health and money into consideration, this attitude of Catherine was madness; and to snap her out of it, not knowing what better she could do, Lapa dragged her off one day to the baths of Vignone, in the Orcia Valley, thinking that some hot baths and meeting people would do her good. Catherine went reluctantly; she insisted, however, upon bathing alone, and, to do penance, instead of getting into the pool where the lukewarm water flowed she got into the pool of hot water where she might meditate upon the sufferings of hell and purgatory.

She herself considered it a miracle that she was not scalded. Defeated, Lapa returned home with her daughter.

Then Catherine caught chicken pox, suffering severely. The mother, tenderly caring for her, had no idea what to do for the sickness. But Catherine assured her mother that she needed just one thing: to assume a habit, that is to become a Dominican tertiary. This was not the first time that Catherine had expressed such desire. However, the *mantellate*, so called because of the black mantle they donned over their white habit when they appeared in public, accepted — at least, in Siena — only widows or elderly women. And Catherine had not been married and was but sixteen years old. Nevertheless, willing to try anything to help her daughter, Lapa went off to the Sisters of Penance to discuss the matter with the prioress, well known to her, for another daughter, Agnes, had joined the order. The prioress already knew of Catherine's aspiration and she was much impressed by the insistence of a girl who wanted to join a community of elderly women, who lived retired lives in their own homes, assembling in their own chapel for prayers and spiritual exercises. "If she is not too pretty," she suggested, "I could look into the matter." So she sent some Sisters, advanced in age and prudence to interview the girl. At that period especially, Catherine's fastings and penances and her sickness had made her physically unattractive. On the other hand she answered the questions of her examiners in a spirit so profoundly religious that the Sisters decided, unanimously, to accept her. Catherine asked the Lord to cure her — and He did.

It seems curious that considering her absorption in God and her yearning to flee the world and conquer her flesh she did not seek admission into a cloistered convent. Instead, Catherine whose only wish was to withdraw from the world, still determined to remain in it. The Lord had called her to a special mission: that of an apostle, whose vocation is to be in the world but not of the world. So in this regard, too, her case was something new and difficult, and in those times hardly conceivable.

The Sisters of Penance, who numbered about ninety in Siena, resided in their own homes but wore the religious habit. They vowed obedience to a prioress, elected by themselves, and depended for spiritual direction upon the Dominican friars of the Church of St. Dominic.

On the appointed day, one Sunday afternoon, she went with her mother to the Church of St. Dominic, so rich in memories, among which were those of St. Thomas Aquinas who had lived in the adjoining friary; and there in the chapel of the Sisters (today known as the chapel delle Volte)² — crowded with the Sisters of Siena, Fra Bartolomeo Montucci invested her with the holy habit, all in black and white, the one symbolizing humility, the other innocence.

Catherine was then sixteen years old — the year was 1363 — but she clearly perceived to what degree the Order of Preachers had tied its spiritual life to the light of Wisdom and centered it in pure Truth, that "sweet truth" the knowledge of which now appeared more than ever as indispensable to the soul: because truth makes the soul humble just as error makes it proud. Furthermore, the culture and the very combativeness of the *Domini canes* — hounds of the Lord — and of the brothers and sisters of Penance, who were originally layfolk living in the married state, enlisted by St. Dominic for his war against the enemies of the Church, had for her a real fascination. She was quite happy.

Now that she was a sister, all her former duties, all her ideals for a life of union, took on more meaning and became more binding. For three years, for the purpose of purifying her mode of thinking, she observed strict silence, interrupted only when she went to confession. She lived between her room and the church. She ate alone, which created no difficulty since she ate no cooked foods except a little bread. She intensified her spiritual common life with the Dominican Order by praying, especially in the hours when the Friars — her "brothers" — slept, reciting in their stead the Divine Office.

Such was her novitiate: the novice master was our Lord Himself, who many times appeared to her and spoke to her heart. At first, hearing the words of her Spouse pronounced clearly and distinctly in the silence of her room, Catherine feared that she was the victim of hallucinations. However, He reassured her, teaching her how to distinguish divine visions from those diabolical: the former begin with bitterness but end in peace; the latter begin with pleasure but end in nausea — just as penances are difficult at first but end in joy, and vices are pleasurable at first but end in bitterness.

There was a period of uninterrupted dialog, in which union became more loving from day to day. Little by little this extraordinary encounter became an ordinary event, so that while she spoke with men her soul was off in contemplation, and not infrequently she was lost in ecstasy. In one of these apparitions, our Lord showed her as in midday brightness the relation between creatures and Creator — a favorite subject of her meditations. Indeed, He imparted to her a theological argument upon the subject, wishing, apparently, to give a solid and universal basis to her spirituality and hence to her apostolate.

On another occasion while she was praying — as she herself related to several spiritual advisers — Jesus Christ appeared to her and asked: "Do you know, daughter, who you are and who I am? If you knew these two things, you would be blessed. You are that which is not; I am He who is. If you have this knowledge in your soul, the enemy can never deceive you; you will escape all his snares; you will never consent to anything contrary to my commandments; and without difficulty you will acquire every grace, every truth, every light."

Catherine's ascent to God is all in this truth: all her enlightenment came from this discovery; her teaching and the secret of her power in dealing with souls proceeded from this idea. She achieved that totality that had made St. Francis exclaim: "My God, my All."

From this basic truth Catherine was to draw wisdom to reform politics and economies, to teach Christian realism to professors and learned men, to sovereigns and popes.

NOTES:  Chapter 3

1. literally: where washing is stretched out to dry.
2. literally: of the vaulted ceilings.

# 4. God and I

With that lesson Catherine became fundamentally learned: she was founded upon a rock; there were no more shadows. *I, nothing; God, All. I, nonbeing; God, Being.* The Almighty had one day made an analogous revelation to Moses on Mount Sinai, amid clouds and thunder; now He repeated it to Catherine in the dimness of a tiny room, amid the silence of a sleeping city. That which is nonbeing receives being, it gets it from God; so that the reason for human existence lies in filling up its own nothingness with the fullness of God, in making itself God by participation, that is by living God, by doing His will, by identifying itself with His mind. Thus, in loving God, it loves itself as it should, for it is His gift.

For Catherine this was a discovery so memorable that from then on she explained it to everyone who would listen: great and small, sovereigns and artisans, summoning all to a knowledge of self lest they be led astray by a world that was unreal and phantasmal — shadow and myth — the world of nonbeing.

The discovery enabled the girl of Fontebranda to remove the barricade of egoism which always impedes progress. Wherefore she became still more ruthless with herself, that is against her bodily senses, her imagination, her passions, and sensual tendencies; this, she was convinced, was true spirituality. Hatred of herself, to love God; merciful toward herself by being cruel to herself. She fought her self-love, seeing that the true love of one's self is a hatred of the I, to leave everything open to God.

This humiliating of herself, this weeping, this annihilation of herself in the conviction of her own nothingness, all served to purify Catherine's soul of every shadow, to make it a limpid crystal, an absolute void through which the light of God passed unhindered.

But how was it that this girl, without any instruction (she still could not read) having no contact with theologians, expressed mystic and dogmatic intuitions, so ingenious that they burst forth like flashes of light, to the admiration and dismay of her contemporaries? The answer is evident: she succceded in being no longer herself, so that Christ might live in her; because becoming completely humble, she was, like Mary, a handmaid of the Lord, a void which the spirit of God made full of grace. And this divine grace made her godlike.

Her instruction was completed by our Lord when He told her one day: "My daughter, think of Me; if you will do this, I shall immediately think of you." Catherine understood: she thought only of Him; and she came to realize how He always thought of her: and in this exchange by which the divine love in a certain sense elevated the creature to the level of the Creator (called forth non-being into being), she saw that love which, if it had made God human, made man godlike. Thenceforward Catherine took no thought at all of what she ate or what she drank or of what happened to her; she left it all to Him. And this conduct of hers became also the norm for her followers.

Thus, much later, one night when she and her followers were in a storm at sea, as to our Lord on the lake, they cried to her for help. Her confessor, Fra Raimondo, anxiously exclaimed: "Mother, do you not see what danger we are in?" But she silenced him: "What does it matter?" She ordered the helmsman to steer in the name of God and to ride with the wind as our Lord sent it. Then everything went so well that the passengers, seeing the change in the sea, were soon chanting the *Te Deum*. Catherine herself explained the secret: "The soul that sees its own nothingness and realizes

the light to discern the danger that threatened her and she fought back with a surge of self-hatred against a temptation to lukewarmness appearing under the guise of sadness. "Have you chosen to serve God in order to enjoy consolations rather than to enjoy Him eternally?" she asked herself contemptuously, and she spurred herself on to add new practices to her customary devotions. She began to visit the church more frequently, prostrating herself in adoration and finding that in the house of God the molestations of the devil had less power over her. But upon returning to her little room she would find it filled with new diabolical foulness: but would pray all the more until the Lord would at length free her. In one of these respites divine enlightenment made clear to her that by means of such temptations our Lord was giving her the grace of fortitude, a thing she had prayed for from the beginning. At last she understood the mystery of temptation.

A demon assailed her, whispering: "Wretched girl, what are you trying to do? Live your whole life in this deplorable condition? If you do not give in to us we shall persecute you to your death." Her soul now tempered by divine enlightenment, this time Catherine replied: "For my joy I have chosen pain, and it is not difficult for me to put up with these and other persecutions of yours in the name of the Saviour, for as long as may please Him; on the contrary I rejoice in them!"

To see her rejoicing in her suffering: this was for the demons a decisive defeat and in humiliation they fled from her. A light from on high filled her little room with brilliance in the midst of which appeared Jesus in agony on the cross. With infinite tenderness He spoke to her: "My daughter, Catherine, do you see how much I have suffered for you? Do not hesitate, then, to suffer for Me." Catherine deeply moved by His calling her — "Catherine, My child" dared a gentle reproof: "My Lord, then where were You when my heart was assailed by such temptations?" "I was in your heart," Jesus replied. "But how could that be," insisted the virgin, with reverent boldness, "when my heart was choked with impure thoughts?" And our Lord explained that since those horrible thoughts caused her not joy but anguish, it was proof that He, hidden in her heart, caused her this suffering; it was His presence that caused the pain. On the contrary, when she promptly offered to submit with all her heart to this test, then the anguish was taken from her; and as it was removed, Christ approached her, appeared to her; furthermore in the future He would appear to her and with greater familiarity, as a reward for the battle that would be won with His power.

Many times Catherine told of this most comforting of the many comforting apparitions of our Lord; and she delighted to be called by Him "My daughter, Catherine" a reminder of the ineffable moment when Love conversed with her.

And so it was. Christ came to her, spoke with her, walked with her in the tiny room, reciting the Psalter with her as if they were friars in choir. On occasion Mary or Dominic or the Magdalen or Peter and Paul accompanied Him, now singly, now in groups. Catherine read the Psalter — at the age of twenty she had learned to read.

One of her sisters in religion, possibly Alessia Savacini, whom thereafter she wished always at her side, had begun to teach her to read; however, she made but little progress until she asked the help of Jesus Himself; then she made rapid strides. The rapidity with which she passed from illiteracy to a knowledge of letters and really expeditious readings seemed to Father Raimondo "a clear evidence of divine intervention."

## 5. Mystical Betrothal

Catherine scaled the way of the cross with rapid steps — just as she had climbed four at a time the stairs of her home; and in this ascent she returned to the house of her Bridegroom. There she waited, as have the great saints, to celebrate the mystical betrothal with Him, repeating the loving invocations of the bride in the Canticle of Canticles. The dark night, with its terrible trials, by means of which to gain paradise she had to pass through hell, and, to purify her love, she had to endure purgatory, had extirpated from her soul even the most subtle traces of human love and indeed of spiritual consolations. Fastened to the cross, nailed there by love, she found herself free at last: all for her Betrothed.

She knew well that, in order not to be expelled as an unworthy servant, she had to present herself for those heavenly nuptials clad in the wedding garment, "The soul must be arrayed in love, with which it can enter into lasting life," she was to write to Ramon, a flax dresser in Florence, determined to dedicate himself to God. And the wedding garment was the vesture of opprobrium, tortures, torments, taunts, and insults freely accepted for love of Him, in perseverance to the end, without becoming weary, without asking respite, with joyful thanksgiving. A prelude to such crucifixion must be a radical renunciation, not merely breaking worldly ties but decisively cutting them off with the knife of hatred and love: of hatred for the old man, of love for God and fellow man.

Catherine's espousal occurred when she was twenty years old, in the flower of her youth, on Shrove Tuesday 1367, when Siena was wildest in its carousals and the populace poured through the streets dancing, singing, ogling, abandoning itself to collective madness. Siena was noted for its elegance, the variety and intensity of its holidays, during which the *brigata spandereccia*, its prodigal band of young dandies, went the limit. Was ever such a foolish gentry as the Sienese? queried Dante.[1] Manners had become increasingly frivolous, and the populace, floundering in economic instability and political ineptitude, sought to drown its bitterness in orgies.

Catherine, perhaps the one citizen of the town completely detached from that carnival madness, kept to that little room, high ceilinged, heavy with silence, into which penetrated only an occasional echo of distant voices, more a lament than merrymaking, only to die there. And she was firmly convinced that hers was the true joy, there in that silence, and that against the noisy background of unthinking youth the only true reality was the crucified Christ: Truth and Love.

"Lord, strengthen my faith!" she prayed again and again in the midst of that insanity of pleasure. "Lord, grant me fullness of faith!" Again and again she repeated the invocation, until at last our Lord appeared to her and called to her in the tender terms He had used before: "Since you alone have rejected all these vanities and for love of Me have fled them and in Me alone have placed all the devotion of your heart, I have determined to celebrate with you the feast of your espousal to Me. . . ."

And while He spoke, from the shadows behind Him emerged the figures of the Blessed Virgin Mary, of St. John the Evangelist and of St. Paul, and then after a moment, David with his harp. Thus began the heavenly feast, of nuptials more joyful and more impressive than any that Siena had ever devised. While the prophet fingered the strings of his harp, releasing soft music in which it seemed all Paradise poured out in song, Jesus Christ ranged Himself at Catherine's side, and in the presence of the two witnesses, apostles of the Faith, He placed a ring upon her finger; then as the angelic choirs paused in silence He pronounced the ritual formula: "I, Your Creator and Your Saviour, wed you in this vow which, until you celebrate with Me in heaven Our eternal nuptials, will preserve you spotless. . . . Armed with the power of this faith you will successfully overcome all your adversaries."

Jesus and Catherine now formed one union. Trembling, Catherine kissed the wedding ring, set with a diamond circled with four pearls. She divined its meaning: faith like a diamond; intention, thought, word and action, pure and precious as pearls. From that moment she never took from her finger that ring, which only her own eyes could see and which even she could not see if for a moment her thoughts strayed from her Bridegroom.

NOTE:   Chapter 5

1. Inferno, XXIX canto.

## II. Contemplation

# 6. The Apostolate

Thus for Catherine was concluded the period of her formation. She had renounced the world, she was united to her Spouse. She had loved God with all her heart, with all her soul, with all her mind: she had fulfilled heroically the first great commandment. Now it remained to carry out the second, like unto the first: Thou shalt love thy neighbor as thyself.

And to love is to serve.

That year, on July 31, died a citizen of Siena who was great in the history of sanctity: the Blessed Giovanni Colombini. Lisa, who was a member of Giovanni's family and who was to become a follower of Catherine, had married one of Lapa's sons. Giovanni Colombini had been a merchant and a political leader who was converted by reading the life of St. Mary of Egypt. He renounced his wealth and seemed like a madman: mad with love of God and of the sick.

That year Giovanni's cousin, the Blessed Catherine Colombini, also the cousin of Lisa Benincasa, inspired by our Catherine's example, had founded the community of Jesuates, modeled upon the male community of the same name instituted by Giovanni Colombini —

two creatures seeking holiness by serving Jesus in His afflicted members.

Our Lord asked Catherine Benincasa, too, to serve her fellow men, to love Him in them, to achieve the full measure of love. He consecrated her the mother of all His sons. It meant that, just when she had achieved supreme renunciation of the world, she must return to the word to participate in all the drama of its tragic incidents in order to love God in men.

And this second oblation — the renunciation, so to speak, of renunciation — Jesus asked of her, to her astonishment, much as the annunciation to the Virgin Mary that she was to become a mother. How could this thing be that a young woman, a sister, set apart from the world, only yesterday unable to read, could become entangled in that swarm of men and women, in which abounded the learned and the powerful, the proud and the wealthy, loose women and ignorant laborers, in a viper's nest of strife and passion, in which so many souls were destroyed? How could it be that she should abandon her quiet cell to walk the streets of the world, when up until now, even when she had to come out for a moment to deal with people her heart was transfixed with pain?

And yet the Lord called her to the observance of the two great commandments — of both of them; so that, as He explained to her, she must walk not with one but with two feet, she must fly with two wings. Had He reminded her of the zeal of her childhood when she longed to dress as a man so as to enter the Order of Preachers — which is assuredly not an order of contemplatives but of fighters — with the intention of serving souls? And was she not now a Dominican? True, but in those times a woman apostle, a tertiary who mixed with the crowds, was unheard of. A woman should be either in the cloister, immersed in silence, or shut up at home.

"How can this thing be?" protested Catherine, like Mary. "How can this thing be, that I, a little nobody, a weakling, can be of use to souls? I am only an insignificant woman."

Catherine's reasoning did try to follow the judgment of her contemporaries, including even directors of conscience. In that man-dominated civilization, albeit Christian, woman was viewed with distrust, especially as regards the Faith. True, in those days men did honor to the courage of Bridget of Vadstena[1] and her daughter Catherine; but these were two aristocrats, come from afar, the innovators of new usages.

At Siena, and in all Italy, on the contrary, it was necessary to remove the vast, stifling featherbed of misogynous distrust before a young woman of the people, without prestige and without the credentials of wealth and culture, could be emancipated. "With Me there is neither man nor woman," our Lord explained to her, "neither commoner nor nobleman; but everyone is equal in My sight." God sees only souls: not sexes, not castes, nor titles. However, this truth, clear in Sacred Scripture, seemed incendiary to those extinguishers of divine love, those who thought it their duty to smother the Holy Spirit wherever His flame appeared, especially if the flame was enkindled, with a rush of fire and blood, in the breast of a woman. But her Spouse was exact in His explanation: "I wish you to know that in this age pride has so increased, particularly among those supposed to be learned and wise, that My sense of justice can tolerate them no longer. I have determined to confound them. Hence I shall give the world women, unlearned and weak, but endowed by Me with virtue and heavenly wisdom, to defeat their boldness. . . ."

Here, then, was Catherine's mission: physically slight, culturally a nobody, to confound the learned, the savants. "Scatter the proud in thy indignation . . ." (Job 40:6).

Fra Raimondo observes: "That which, in my opinion, is most to be wondered at, is this abundance of graces which in our days God had given in such profusion to the weaker sex, to women, to confound the pride of men, especially those men who, swollen up with self-esteem, are convinced that they are wise. . . . It is these men, it seems to me, that the Eternal Wisdom has wished to confound with the humble wisdom and the prodigious works of holy young women, so that no man may exalt himself before God."

"You, therefore," Jesus told Catherine, "must in future be most obedient, against the time when I shall determine to send you out in public. I shall never abandon you, wherever you may be." Catherine's faith was strong; she bowed her head in submission.

Then Jesus recited the Divine Office with her again and, as the hour struck, said to her: "Go, it is time for dinner, and your family will be going to the table. Go, be with them, and then come back to Me." With them, His creatures, and then with Him, their Creator: the two commandments in practice.

Catherine had learned her lesson; she was prepared for revolutionary action. She paid no heed to her own weakness, but with the light of reason strengthened by the light of faith she believed. Later on the Eternal Father Himself would confirm these illuminations: It is much better to go, for counsel about the salvation of one's soul, to a simple person who is humble, but with an upright and holy conscience, than to a man who is learned but proud, profound in studies and steeped in knowledge, because such latter person cannot give what he hasn't got, and always runs the risk of losing in the darkness of his life the light of Sacred Scripture.

This wisdom of the servants of God, even if they are unlearned, is not a confused groping in the dark, but the true light at which one arrives through love, at which one arrives through reason. And this truth our saint will proclaim convincingly. The light of reason is our first participation in the nature of God, the true Light, and it is integrated with the light of faith: faith to be practiced with reason; reason to be enlightened with faith.

Thus appears a second phase of Catherine's life: the phase of active life; but not as a change or turning point in her former life — rather as its increase and complement. She merely joined action to contemplation; or, more exactly, her contemplation was so penetrating that it had to express itself in action. She was united to God; therefore she had to be united to men. And if she will no longer live enclosed in a cell with walls, she will always live in the cell which is knowledge of self. She will carry her cloister, her cell, with her wherever she goes; her rule will ever be love.

Thus we can see how all Catherine's ascetical and mystical preparation was simply training to enable her to transform the love of God also into the love of men. A light had been kindled; it could no longer be hidden. "I do not intend to separate you from Me," our Lord told her; "on the contrary, I desire to draw you, to draw you to Myself more strongly by means of your love of neighbor."

Meanwhile to draw her more strongly, He aroused in her a devouring hunger for the Eucharist, so that she wished when possible to receive every day; and this at a time when frequent communion, not to say daily communion, was not practiced, and the ecclesiastical authorities, from motives of "humility," frowned upon the idea of approaching frequently this "fearsome" sacrament.

NOTE:  Chapter 6

1. St. Bridget of Sweden, who after her husband's death founded at Vadstena, the Brigittine order, or Order of the Saviour, for men and women.

## 7. Servant of the Servants

Catherine's active life began in the ways suggested by Jesus and followed the pattern of Christian asceticism: she started out with the members of her family and on the humblest level — in the kitchen. She returned to the kitchen as a servant. And when the family cook was ill, Catherine, while performing all the kitchen duties also helped the family maid, assisting her with love, and gladly making herself literally servant of the servants, to the point where she became enamored of the name and made it her own — "I, Catherine, servant and slave of the servants of Jesus Christ. . . ."

Since she busied herself about the house with Christ ever in her heart, she realized still more that cleaning up the kitchen or sweeping and dusting the rooms became a prayer, a doing of His will, and eventually a participating in His life. She loved Him with such rapture that many a time, in the midst of household chores, she was lost in ecstasy; she felt her soul momentarily to be on the point of leaving the earth. In these transports the members of her body experienced no sensation; her hands were folded together inseparably; her eyes stared; her neck was as rigid as marble. One day when her mother came upon her in one of these states, frightened she tried to straighten her neck; she desisted only when a companion shouted at her to stop lest she injure her daughter. In fact, when Catherine came to, her neck pained her severely. Another day she was seized in ecstasy at the kitchen fireplace while intent upon operating the roasting spit. The spit stopped and Catherine, entranced, seemed turned to stone. Fortunately there was present one who loved and admired her — Lisa, who silently took her sister-in-law's place at the work, turning the spit and then later going about the business of putting the other rooms in order. When she returned to the kitchen later on she discovered that Catherine, in her ecstasy, had fallen across the burning brands in the fireplace. "Heaven help us," she cried out, "Catherine has been burned!" And she hastened to drag her to safety. However, though the fire was burning away, she could find no burns on Catherine's body nor did she detect the odor of burning clothes or flesh. Neither Catherine's face, nor her hands, nor her garments had been touched by the fire. And yet Catherine must have lain for some time on the burning brands.

And the miracle of which we have just spoken was repeated on other occasions. One day in church while, lost in ecstasy, Catherine fell on a candle flame, burning off her white veil. Lisa, Alessia, Francesca, and other companions who came upon her with the flame licking her head were dismayed, but soon realized better than ever with what power they were confronted. A disciple of hers, Gabriele, of the noble Piccolomini family of Siena, saw her fall upon a burning brazier, from which she rose, unharmed, to exclaim: "Malatasca, Malatasca!" Malatasca in the Tuscan dialect means *devil*.

At this time she took part in the life of her family, even to the point of concerning herself with their political and financial probblems. The Benincasa family belonged to the well-to-do element of the city; indeed one of its members for the two months' period of September and October, 1367, was a member of the Tribunal of Twelve.[1] However, among the Twelve, the magistracy, the middle classes, and merchants had imposed upon the nobles, an arrangement ratified by Emperor Charles IV, and a crude civil war was in progress — one of those endless conflicts in which the liberty of the commune was being frittered away amid economic difficulties attended by ruinous epidemics. In one episode of that internecine warfare, when members of the Benincasa family, together with some other members of their faction, found it necessary to seek asylum[2] in the church of St. Anthony, Catherine came to their assistance. Convinced that this church did not offer asylum sufficiently secure, she convoyed her brothers to the Hospice of La Scala, clear across the city; no one dared move a finger against her protégés. Furthermore, she had foreseen correctly; those who had taken refuge at St. Anthony's were taken captive and most of them were killed.

Although the members of her own family were the chief objects of her concern, little by little, she passed on to the service of the poor — always the principal school of the saints. After all, also the poor belonged to her family: God was their Father and Mary their Mother.

She served the poor in all sorts of ways, in all their material and spiritual necessities. As to material assistance, being bound by the vow of poverty, she had little or nothing of her own to give, but she got leave from her father to give the poor whatever was in the Benincasa home. Her largess, however, was governed by prudent discretion; she sought out the most needy and, among these, those who were ashamed to beg. Each morning, setting out on her first works of charity, bearing a cargo of bread, wine, oil, and other supplies, she climbed the stairs of the poor, opened their rickety doors, left her gifts and, being careful not to make her presence known, moved on to other hovels.

She was able to do this because as a tertiary, she was not obliged to conventual residence. Here was a new possibility in monasticism, we may call it public monasticism, religious life, not distinct, but fused and infused in the life of the world.

Knowing well enough the soul of Catherine, we may be sure that she pushed her charity to heroic lengths. We are told, for example, that one morning, at dawn, she rose from her bed, although she was enervated by a swollen condition of her whole body, to give assistance to the family of a widow. She was weighted down with a sack of grain, a demijohn of wine, a flask of oil and various comestibles, all of which made a burden too great for her strength. Still she carried the load, carried along herself by the ardor of her love for the poor, by the love of Christ present in the poor. The way was too long, and eventually her strength failed her as her fever mounted. She begged her Spouse to help her; painfully she was able to reach the doorsill of a hovel. She pushed open the unlocked door and in silence deposited her burden in the dark room. The widow living there, however, woke from sleep and rushed over to her. Catherine tried to flee but much to her confusion, she realized that she could not rise from the sill. So again, she besought her Spouse: "Why, my loving Master, do You mock me? Does it seem fitting to You to mock me and gibe at me by holding me here? Give me back my strength, I beg You; let me get back to my home."

Then, addressing herself to her enfeebled body she declared: "I must walk, even though I die in the attempt!"

Her will was formidable; and at its command, her body responded to some extent. Down on all fours, she started to move away, not, however, before the widow, approaching, recognized her from her religious habit. Calling forth all her reserve strength, Catherine finally succeeded in dragging herself to her cell before full daylight and there, she collapsed upon her wooden pallet.

On another occasion while she was praying in the chapel of the volate, a beggar asked her for an alms. Herself, a sister in a mendicant Order, she had nothing of her own to give him, so she asked him to wait until she could return to her home.

"I cannot wait," the man insisted.

Catherine detached the little silver cross from her rosary and gave it to the beggar, who went off happily. The next night, while she was praying, her Spouse appeared to her with the little silver cross in His hand — only now it sparkled with gems. "My daughter, do you recognize this cross?" He asked her. "Certainly, only when it was mine it was by no means so beautiful." And our Lord said: "You gave it to me yesterday in a burst of charity, which is signified in these precious stones. And I promise you that on the day of judgment I shall present it to you as it is now, so that your joy will be filled in the sight of angels and men. The thing shall not be hidden — I will not permit it — when I shall exalt the mercy and the justice of the Father, this work of mercy that you have done for Me."

Yet another extraordinary jest our Lord indulged in one day when she was engaged with a sister companion in the chapel of her Order. As she descended the stairs to leave, a young pilgrim, apparently a little more than thirty years old, asked her for a garment to wear. It was cold and he was thinly dressed. "Wait a moment, my good man," she replied. With her companion, she climbed back to the chapel, where she took off the sleeveless tunic which she wore under her outer robe in winter, and returning to the pilgrim she held it out to him. He took it, but persisted: "My lady, since you have provided me with a woolen garment, won't you please give me one of linen, too?" "Follow me," she said, "and I shall give you what you ask." She went to her home and from the closet where her father's and brother's clothes were kept, she drew forth a pair of drawers and an undershirt, and smilingly she offered them to the beggar. But the young man did not move; he eyed her with a petulant air. "My lady, what can I do with this sleeveless garment?" Unruffled and happily Catherine set about rummaging through wardrobes in search of a pair of woolen sleeves to go with the tunic. But she could find none. Then her eyes fell upon a dress belonging to the family servant. Catherine took it from the hook where it was hanging, cut the threads that joined the sleeves to the garment and, still smiling, she gave them to the beggar.

The man thanked her, but still lingered on. He began to tell her about the plight of a companion, no less needy than himself, who was going about badly in need of clothing. What was she to do? She could not give away any more clothing from her home, for the whole family, with the exception of her father, had rebelled at her generosity and had forbidden her to touch anything of theirs. She had only one garment left — her own. Could she give the beggar that? Her charity said "yes," but her modesty said "no": "I would give you my habit," she told the beggar . . . "but I cannot." "I know," he replied, smiling; and saluting her, he departed.

The following night he appeared to Catherine while she prayed in her cell. She had already suspected who He was. Now she recognized Him, as He presented her with her tunic, now embroidered with pearls and other precious stones. Then there developed a conversation between the two during which Catherine was invested in a tunic that was to protect her from every sort of cold, whether of body or of soul, until at last she would don the vesture of eternal glory; a tunic which she saw our Lord draw from the wound in His side, all stained with His blood, radiant symbol of vesture eternal. From that day this tunic covered her body summer and winter, protecting her from every change of temperature.

On another day, glancing from her little window into the street below she discovered a half-clothed beggar sleeping huddled against a wall. The sight moved her and impelled her to go to his aid; it was, however, time for recitation of the Divine Office, so she drew the window curtains and started to read the psalms. But during the reading she did not see Jesus Christ. She saw the beggar in whom she should see Jesus. ". . . inasmuch as you did this to one of these least brethren of mine, you did it to me. . . . For I was hungry and you gave me to eat. . . . I was naked, and you covered me" (Mt. 25:36). These assertions of the Saviour leaped from the verses of the prophet and distracted her until at length it seemed clear that the Lord awaited her there in rags, lying in the deserted street. She arose and went into the kitchen, took a loaf of bread and went out to lay it next to the sleeping outcast. The beggar, however, awakened and, thanking her, asked if she did not have some clothing to give him. Catherine had nothing left of her own; and she had been forbidden to give away anything more from the house. So she took off the mantle she was wearing and gave it to him. And once again, in the middle of the night, Jesus returned to thank her and to reward her, investing her this time with a special grace due to which she could thenceforward go forth without the protection of her mantle, even in the depth of winter, without feeling any cold.

We need not be surprised to see this Benincasa girl, wholly trusting in God, also working miracles of multiplying food and drink. As when, not wanting to give the poor wine from a certain cask that had begun to turn sour, from which, however, her own family were still drinking, she broached another cask in which the wine was still good. She passed out the wine liberally among the poor and then began to serve her family from this same cask. What with parents, children, relatives, grandchildren, and guests, the Benincasa family used up a cask of wine in a fortnight. This cask, however, was still giving wine a month later, both for the family and guests of Catherine (the poor) and for the family and guests of her father, Giacomo. None had ever drunk a wine so excellent, although the Tuscan hills thereabout were noted for their exquisite product. Though her family was not quite happy about the matter, Catherine passed out wine more liberally to her growing clientele of the streets, to whom a glass of clear white wine was a treat for the stomach and a source of joy and well-being. A second month passed, and then a third, until at last, with the coming of harvest time, it was necessary to cleanse and prepare all casks to receive the newly crushed fruit of the vine. A workman took up Catherine's inexhaustible cask, with the idea of transferring what wine was left to another receptacle, but when the bung was started not even a drop of wine came forth, and when the interior of the cask was examined it was as dry as if for months it had touched no liquid; although on the very evening before a large flask of sparkling and exquisite wine had been filled from it!

NOTES: *Chapter 7*

1. The rule of the nobles in Siena had become so tyrannical that in 1277 it was decreed that no patrician could occupy the chief magistracy; power was to remain in the hands of the middle classes and merchants. The size of the magistracy — which had varied from 24 to 36 members was reduced to 15 in 1280, and seven years later to nine. In the early years of the fourteenth century there were many minor riots and battles, and in 1355 when the Emperor Charles IV passed through Siena he gave his blessing to an irregular government of 12 which had been set up by reformers against the nine.

2. From the fourth century and throughout the Middle Ages, Christian churches were places of *asylum* — i.e., refuge where persons could not be molested by the civil authorities.

# 8. The Infirm

Another goal of Catherine's steps through the city was Siena's hospitals. In Siena various hospitals had been established by Christian piety: they were all-purpose institutions for social stress of every sort: the sick, the invalids, needy pilgrims, beggars, whose presence had the healthy effect of developing among the Sienese — quarrelsome as they were, and frivolous and inclined to a sort of selfish materialism — more generous sentiments, awakening in them the consciousness of brotherhood. Catherine made herself the nurse of her sick sisters and of the abandoned poor in general.

We may recall the loving services she performed for a certain Tecca, a patient in the hospital of S. Lazzaro, a leprosarium, just outside the Porta Romana. Leprosy in those days inspired a particular horror because, while the healthy ran grave danger of contracting it, there was no known cure for those afflicted with it. Tecca had the disease in an advanced stage; she was wretchedly poor and without friends. So Catherine every day, morning and evening, visited the woman to bring her food and drink and to serve her in every possible way. Abandoned by all, as ignorant as she was miserable, poor Tecca, instead of admiring and thanking this angel

47

of mercy, by a sort of perversion, not too unusual in weak minds, little by little, convinced herself that she had a right to all this attention and this service. She began to order Catherine about, then to be arrogant, and finally abusive. She was the placable mistress dealing with a servant. For instance, if Catherine would be a bit late in coming some morning, because in church her ecstatic prayers had been somewhat longer, Tecca would greet her with sarcastic abuse: "Welcome, at last, madame, queen of Fontebranda![1] And what was her highness doing so long in church? Spending the whole morning with the friars? It seems that her highness can never get enough of those priests!" Catherine attempted no reply to these insulting insinuations. Rather she tried to placate the old leper, reassuring her: "I shall hasten to do anything that you need of me." Graciously and efficiently she went about lighting the fire, hanging the pot over the brazier, preparing a meal.

This went on for a long time, so that Lapa, torn with fear, at length ventured to reprove her vigorously both for running the risk of contracting the disease and for making herself the servant of this leprous virago. So Catherine had also to calm her mother, reminding her of the example set by our Lord. Inevitably, she did contract the disease. First her hands became infected; which did not disturb her, serene as she was in the conviction that her existence did not belong to her but to God and hence to the sick and the poor in whom Jesus dwelt. The affair ended with the leper's death. Catherine assisted her spiritually and corporally during her last agony; after her death Catherine washed the repellent body, dressed it carefully and, after the funeral Mass, buried it with her own hands. Immediately after Tecca's burial, Catherine's hands were healed.

Another strange type of infirmity Catherine found in a fellow member of the Dominican Third Order, a woman called Palmarina, a devoted widow who had given herself and all her possessions to the Hospital della Misericordia. By reason of her dedication, she conceived herself to be a heroine of sanctity and she nourished a sordid envy of Catherine who, although without having married and without having given lavishly to the hospital, was much more highly esteemed by all. So with unctious deception Palmarina began to scatter evil charges against Catherine's virtue — an insinuation here, a plausible calumny there — apparently convinced that she was laboring for the glory of God in heaven by slandering a daughter of His upon earth. Catherine's first reaction was characteristic of her; she sought to win over this sister to a more objective practice of brotherly love; and with this in mind she proffered her a whole series of services, all unrequited and unappreciated. Eventually the unfortunate woman became seriously ill and took to her bed. Her condition, however, instead of recalling her to the duties of fraternal charity, increased her malice and gave new cutting edges to her tongue. Catherine went often to visit her, taking her gifts and assisting her in all sorts of ways, trying to show that she loved her, but Palmarina ordered her servant to show Catherine to the door. The patient went from bad to worse, until she was at the point of death. Still, however, enmeshed in her hatred for Catherine, she would not or she could not ask for the sacraments, and was in grave danger of dying in sin.

When Catherine was informed of the situation, she plunged into prayer for the salvation of that soul. Kneeling in her bare little cell she remonstrated with Christ: "O Lord, have I been born so that through my fault souls created to Your image should go down to hell?" As usual she blamed herself for the evil that befell others. Had it not been for her, Palmarina would not have fallen into temptation: it were better never to have been born than to become the cause of ruin to souls redeemed by the blood of Christ. And in this case there was question of a fellow religious toward whom she was bound by special ties of duty and affection. Her tormented mind reached a drastic decision: she would not stop calling upon the infinite goodness of God until He had transformed into good all the evil she had merited and Palmarina would be freed from eternal death. Although our Lord then revealed to her the wickedness of the dying woman and explained to her the divine necessity of punishing a hatred so inveterate, prostrate in tears she still begged Him to save that soul. "Otherwise, I shall not leave this room except as a corpse. Punish me, O Lord, for her sins!"

For three days and nights the agony of Palmarina continued, a rebel against the Spouse because an enemy of the virgin. At last, with her tears and her pleading, Catherine conquered the Unconquerable and overcame the Omnipotent, as her biographer remarks: Palmarina, illumined by divine grace, recognized her sin, asked pardon, received the sacraments and died a happy death. Catherine had a vision of that soul's salvation, and from that time onward she received from the Saviour a special gift — the power of seeing the beauty or the ugliness of souls, so that she might, with this advantageous knowledge, work for their benefit. Thenceforward to her sense of smell the virtue of a soul came as a perfume; vice, as a stench. Particularly remarkable was this new-found sensitivity during the period of her public mission, for she was able to detect, even at a great distance, centers of moral infection. Confronted by a person with an evil conscience, Catherine experienced a visible nausea, and could not look directly at the unfortunate being; when she was unable to avoid a conversation, she would ask the sinner first to cleanse his conscience, and then she would talk with him.

There was also another of her sisters-in-religion who repaid Catherine's services to her with treachery. This one was called (according to the Sienese custom) by the masculine name of Andrew; she was suffering from cancer of the breast. Now at the last stages of the disease, her breast was a fetid sore, and almost no one came to visit her; she lay unattended on her filthy couch in an evil-smelling room. Precisely because the sick woman was so abandoned by everybody, Catherine reserved to herself the duty of assisting her, which she did with patience, joy, and love inspired by heaven. Her youth and her graciousness brought a breath of peace into the desolation of the stricken creature, astonished at her heroism. Catherine's heroism was such that one day, having removed the dressing from the ulcer and nauseated by the odor, she was so impatient with herself and by the reaction of her stomach to the misery of a creature redeemed by the blood of Christ that she determined to punish herself, and forthwith pressed her face to the diseased breast and held it there until she had overcome her nausea.

The mind of the sick woman, already troubled, became completely upset: she began to suspect that the girl was abnormal, guilty of aberrations. She could not bring herself to believe that a normal young woman would thus serve an old, cancerous wreck, in a fetid cell. She decided that Catherine must be morally evil and so, instead of gratitude she began to develop a sort of hatred for her, under the influence of which to the few persons who came to visit her, even for a moment, she began to speak slanderously of her. As defaming gossip got around, some of the older nuns determined to find out what it was all about; they questioned the sick woman, got from her the details of Catherine's alleged misconduct even to the point of breaking her vow of virginity. The young woman, humble and patient under the charges, made but one reply to them: "I assure you, my sisters, that by the grace of Jesus Christ, I am a virgin."

Catherine continued unremittingly her care of the sick woman; at the feet of Christ, however, she wept bitterly, for close to her heart were cleanness of heart and the name of being a virgin consecrated to Him. Then our Lord appeared to her, holding out to her with one hand a crown of gold and with the other a crown of thorns, and He bade her choose one of the two for this life, reserving the other for the life to come. Of course, Catherine chose the crown of thorns; and she pressed it tightly upon her head so as to feel the pain.

When the evil gossip reached the ears of Catherine's mother, Lapa's anger knew no bounds. Seeking out her daughter she demanded: "Didn't I always tell you not to serve that foul old woman? Here are the thanks you get! Her evil tongue has dishonored you in the sight of all your sisters. If you continue to visit her and to serve her I shall no longer recognize you as my daughter!" In silence Catherine heard her out. Then, after a pause, she approached her mother, still trembling with rage, and knelt down before her. Then gently she began to recall for her mother the sufferings that Jesus Christ underwent for love of us, in the midst of all the ingratitude and blasphemies of the very ones He came to save. Was she to abandon that old woman, to leave her alone to die a horrible death?

Lapa, after all, was a Christian; deeply moved, she allowed herself to be persuaded by her daughter — whom she now blessed: that daughter who never ceased to amaze her and to confound her with conduct unheard of. So Catherine went back to assisting the old woman whose malignancy devoured her little by little while her conscience, enlightened now by the heroism of the virgin, gradually awakened her to repentance. At length she saw Catherine as an angel, bright with heavenly light; she begged her pardon and with a loud voice, proclaimed to all the girl's innocence.

On another day as she dressed the ulcer, Catherine experienced such nausea that she was about to faint. But she commanded her spirit to control her flesh. Addressing her body she exclaimed, "Now that which you abhor so much will enter into you!" And she drank from the dish in which she had just washed the open sore.

When our Lord appeared to her He showed His divine pleasure at the act by which she had overcome nature.

Her attitude toward the sick came from her extraordinary ability to see men and things in God, and to make every act a part of the divine economy; everything a person does and everything he says through the instrumentality of man (by "means" of man, as the Sienese have it), he does to God and for God. To all appearances one takes care of a leper, administers to a cancerous patient; in reality he is rendering honor to God. And it is always back to God that Catherine brings events and discussions, so that her every day is a fabric of prayer. Nothing is lost, nothing is wasted; every pain wins merit, every service leads to Christ; one need only suffer and act according to the will of God. Everything becomes religion. Dealing with man, one deals with God; going to work, one goes toward God. "If you see your brother, you should see the Lord," said the first Christians, condensing into a proverb the great double commandment.

NOTE:  *Chapter 8*

1. Fontebranda is the district of Siena, around the Church of St. Dominic, in which Catherine lived.

## 9. Jesus and Catherine

We may say that by the very impetus of love, Catherine's soul had rent the veil that withholds from man's sight the vision of God, and that she now saw Jesus Christ and established contact with the blessed in heaven even here below. Not only the gift of ecstasies, which were for her the ravishings of love during which her lips were often smiling and her eyes filled with tears, but also the gift of seeing distant happenings, enriched her sanctity. She could read men's minds and see beyond walls. One of her brothers who had gone abroad fell into bad habits and upon his return she recounted his sins to him; not only had she seen them from afar but they made his very presence before her like a breath of corruption.

One morning when she was sick Friar Tommaso della Fonte, in whom she confided, came to visit her. "Father," she asked him suddenly, "what were you doing yesterday at three o'clock in the morning?" The Dominican made a gesture of surprise. "I shall tell you, exactly," she went on, "You were writing at that hour." "Really," objected the priest, "really, I was not writing." "True; you were not writing with your own hand; you were dictating to a companion who was taking down what you were saying."

Confounded, the priest asked her: "And what was being written on those pages?" With a twinkle of her eye she replied: "You were describing the singular graces which God in His mercy has seen fit to give this useless servant."

In this episode we can see how even priests and theologians were at last convinced that they were in the presence of something portentious. The fourteenth century, the age of Boccaccio and of Chaucer, was not an epoch of credulity; indeed, the career of Catherine of Siena took place in the midst of the most critical unbelievers and skeptics. All around her lived those spirits who were intellectually awake and psychologically perceptive: not infrequently they were pleasure-loving and profligate; sometimes they were downright immoral. Yet all of them, one after another, admitted the reality. It is easy to deny miracles and visions: the simple truth is that Catherine, whose intelligence was limpid, keen, and vast, saw God, and received from her visions a norm of conduct that cannot be otherwise explained, and with that norm a vigor of action that could not humanly be reconciled with her wretched health; while to the benefits miraculously obtained those benefited gave unanimous testimony and their number increased day by day.

Confronting all denials and objections stands the historical reality called Catherine of Siena, whose power was now about to manifest itself beyond her native city and its environs. Her religious sisters now all believed in her, her confessors were convinced as were persons in circles which continually grew larger. The secretary to whom Fra Tommaso was dictating that night was a flesh-and-blood Dominican called Fra Bartolomeo Dominici, somewhat of an historical figure who, moreover, wished to make the acquaintance of that privileged creature. A few days after the incident his opportunity came. It may be that he wished to clear up some doubt in his mind about Catherine's asserted clairvoyance. And Catherine, receiving him affectionately as a brother in St. Dominic, graciously and ingenuously told him what she had seen the previous evening in the cell of the Prior: she had seen, she said, three friars and she named them one by one. They were discussing a subject, which she also named. And she added: "I always stay awake and pray for you until your monastery bell sounds Matins. If you had good eyes you could see me as I see you, each one of you in particular. I see where you are and what you are doing."

Thus the young nun made a tremendous impression upon him, an impression which he revealed later on. "When I made her acquaintance, she was young and so was I. Her countenance was lovely; her manner, gay. Yet in her presence I felt none of the self-consciousness which I always experienced in the presence of other girls. On the contrary, the more I talked with her, the more all human passions died in my heart."

And this was another sign of Catherine's holiness: she was a woman in whom femininity, in some sense made immaculate by grace, aroused in men a longing for purity; she inspired sentiments that were no doubt aroused by the virgin beauty of Mary. Because she was pure, she evoked purity. Penances, mortifications, ecstasies, recollection, gave her no appearance of severity or aloofness: her smile was spontaneous as a child's; her eyes in the dark shade of heavy lashes were transparent as an angel's; everything about her had an irresistible grace. She loved little children, and embraced them naturally; she was fond of flowers, and cared for them in her father's garden, often weaving them into little crosses which she would send, by Fra Tommaso, to friends of hers as messages from their sisters in Christ. Her singing voice was thin, but pleasing and in tune; and she liked poetry.

To hear her speak was a delightful experience. And she spoke of naught but God. There fell from her lips no idle talk: she belonged to God entirely, and she would not be concerned with aught else. And when she did mention some other subject, it was because she saw all other things in God — the things of the Church, for instance, or the good of souls. These talks of hers were a constant inspiration to her sisters in religion, happy now to be her disciples, as well as to others who now began to attend upon her. Among her sisters we find frequent mention of Lisa, Alessia, Francesca Gori (also a widow), Caterina di Ghetto, Giovanna di Capo, and Caterina dello Spedaluccio. Among the others, besides Fra Raimondo da Capua, Fra Tommaso, and Fra Bartolomeo — all Do-

minicans — there was another, who also became her biographer, Fra
Antonio di Nacci Capparini, of the Dominican Friary of Camporeg-
gio, who, as far back as 1366, had been a dinner guest of the Benincasa family, had met Catherine, had eaten bread baked by her (he
kept a fragment as one would keep a relic), and had been astounded
to hear her discussions about God. Then there was another Dominican, Niccolo di Bindo da Cascina who, attracted by her growing
reputation, and determined to make her acquaintance came upon
her in ecstasy, raised some feet above the floor; out of devotion he
tried with his finger to separate her clasped hands, and for the next
forty-eight hours the finger gave off an indescribable perfume.

From her early years, Catherine had been accustomed to speak of
God, without ever tiring, as a lover would speak of his beloved,
always thinking of her. She slept less than anyone else for her
heart really kept vigil. Sometimes her confessor and disciple, Fra
Raimondo da Capua, hearing her confession toward the end of the
day would doze off and she would arouse him: "Awake, good man!
For the sake of sleep will you lose what is good for your soul? Do I
speak of God to you . . . or to a wall?"

The name of Jesus, falling from her lips, took on the sweetness
of a melody: there was a note, ever new, of attractiveness about
it; those who heard her repeat the sacred name themselves became
enamored of it. "Gesù dolce . . . Gesù amore! . . . O dolce Dio
amore!"

Fra Raimondo tells us of the immense consolation Catherine derived from talking with her eternal Spouse: when she could do so,
she "appeared much more youthful, robust and jovial; while when
she could not, she became weak and almost lifeless." Jesus was her
life: He was its poetry and its force, its beginning and its end.

In the midst of this ravishing union with God and of service to
the poor and the sick, just as she was beginning the formation of
her first disciples, one day in the torrid summer of 1368, she lost
her best friend, the soul she most resembled: her father, Giacomo,
now burdened with years but even more well laden with merits.
He had worked and worried and suffered much during all that girlhood of hers that had sprung up about him like a strange and

impetuous flowering plant; and he had seen in Catherine — among all his other children and daughters-in-law and other relatives — a soul endowed by God with special privileges. Now he was about to leave them all, as one who had completed his task and sought retirement of his master. Catherine remained at his pillow right up to the end to arouse in him joyous expectation of the imminent vision of God, while she prayed and besought her Spouse that she might satisfy for whatever temporal punishment to which her father might be liable, freeing him thus from the pain of Purgatory. She joyfully accepted the bodily sufferings which our Lord sent her. Her father's body was buried August 22 in the crypt of the Church of St. Dominic, where every day the religious chanted the Divine Office.

A month later, on September 24, 1368, the Salimbeni family, with partisans of the Twelve, by force of arms opened the gates of the city to the imperial legate, Malatesta di Malatesta, and his soldiers, who then dominated Siena, house by house. A few days later the emperor himself, Charles IV with his empress, arrived and were guests of the Salimbeni, who had now made themselves head of the people's faction. The royal guests, however, had hardly left the city when an insurrection broke out which overthrew the government; and when, in December, the emperor returned, such tumults broke out that, powerless and mortified, he was compelled to abandon the hostile city, leaving behind him in the first month of 1369, nothing but anarchy. The following year, because of the economic depression, the brothers of Catherine, Bartolomeo and Stefano, went to seek their fortunes in Florence; but even in that center of cloth craftsmanship, unemployment was the order of the day, and the entire Benincasa family was compelled to move out of the traditional residence in Fontebranda.

The entire Christian world was now in the midst of political convulsions which were bringing in their wake ruinous economic consequences.

Wars between kings and political adventurers, inevitably accompanied by epidemics and widespread want, brought about a decadence of democracy and internally and externally prevented any serious coalition for forces for a crusade against the Mohammedan

Crescent which all generous spirits of the time ardently desired.

In the midst of all that sound and fury, Catherine did not lose her calm self-possession; rather the hectic events seemed to strengthen her character to dominate events around her and to direct them all to Christ. As a matter of fact there came a time in which she seemed to realize her childhood dream; to live as a man among men. "Forget about your sex," the Saviour expressly commanded her; so she changed her way of life; she no longer fled the company of men and women; she no longer hesitated for fear of scandalizing the narrow-minded; she determined to follow "manfully" her inspiration: a man's program of action.

## 10. The Deifying Transformation

During one of her frequent ecstasies, Catherine was heard to repeat the phrase: Vidi arcana Dei (I have seen the hidden things of God). And when she came to, she continued to repeat the phrase. When her confessor asked her to explain its meaning, she replied: "I cannot put into words what I have seen." So far, as we may judge, she had been vouchsafed a vision of divinely profound truth, closer than ever to the life of the Holy Trinity Itself, from which she was later on to draw the most extraordinary powers for her mission among men.

On the feast of St. Margaret, Queen of Scots (June 10, 1370) it seemed to her that her heart had penetrated the breast of her Spouse, so as to form but one heart with that of Jesus.

It is symptomatic that the phase of passing from a life hitherto of complete retirement to a life of public action was for the Sienese mystic also a period of the highest contemplation: a total losing of herself in the Eternal in order to be able to operate in the temporal as pure energy of God, as the express wish of Christ. The month from July 17 to August 18, 1370, marks a most intense transformation of her soul, which had now arrived at mystical death to begin dynamic life. That which for other pious souls is the second conversa-

tion, was for her transformation in Christ: she had become the visible expression of her Spouse.

Now, too, at the beginning of each day of ecstasy, there was the reception of Holy Communion. "Father, I am hungry! For the love of God, give me the Food of my soul!" she would beg her confessor. And for weeks on end that was the only food she took even for her body; if she touched any other food, she was not able to retain it. Her brothers and sisters in religion criticized her for this daily approach to the Eucharistic table since, in the fourteenth century, daily Communion was looked upon with suspicion. As a matter of fact, obstacles were thrown in the way of Catherine's receiving Communion, even when this was her only food.

During the night of July 17, 1370, while she was at her prayers, it was revealed to her that on the morrow she would be able to receive Holy Communion. She began her preparation and forthwith her soul seemed to be inundated with blood and fire. With morning came an unusually severe attack of her customary malaise making it impossible for her to move. Yet she remained absolutely certain that she would receive our Lord in the Eucharist. And it turned out that there came a moment when by rallying her forces she could get up and move, though with difficulty, to the Church. There she remembered that her superiors — she always obeyed them as God's representatives — had forbidden her to receive Holy Communion from just any priest who offered Mass. Only Fra Tommaso, her confessor, could give her permission to receive; so she found herself wishing that he would be on hand to say Mass. As a matter of fact, Fra Tommaso was there but, unaware of her presence, he was not of a mind to offer Mass that day. Suddenly, however, he conceived a burning desire to say Mass; donning the sacred vestments he went to an altar which was not his accustomed one. It was the altar near which Catherine, hidden from sight, prayed and awaited his presence. So she received Holy Communion after all. As Fra Tommaso placed the Sacred Host upon her tongue he saw that her face was illumined with a new and extraordinary splendor. In fact she confessed to him on the following day that at that moment of receiving the Body and Blood of her Spouse, her eyes had lost their sight and she could

see nothing but the love of God. Resolutely determined to tear herself away from all created things, which now seemed to her "*uno stomachevole sterco*" — nauseating refuse — she understood as never before the joys of things spiritual and prayed Christ to take from her the last traces of her own will. He heard her prayer, for from that moment her character takes on an imperturbable equilibrium in the face of any and every eventuality.

That day there was consummated the mystical assimilation of Catherine with Christ. Between them took place an exchange of hearts. *Create in me a clean heart, O God* (Psalm 50) she prayed fervently in the Liturgy. And our Lord appeared and took from her her heart. She actually felt that she was without it for two days, that is, until July 20, when the Lord appeared to her, holding a heart which he inserted into her left side, saying: "Here, My dearest daughter, just as I took your heart from you, now I give you Mine, with which you will live." From that moment, Catherine used a new form of prayer: "Lord, I give Thee Thy Heart."

From childhood Catherine had always been earnestly devoted to St. Mary Magdalene. She felt herself filled with sins and she loved that penitent sinner; about all she loved Mary Magdalene's love for Jesus Christ. So on the Magdalene's feast day, July 22, Catherine had a vision of the Lord in the company of His Blessed Mother and of Mary Magdalene. "Whom do you choose?" Christ asked her: "whom do you choose, yourself or Me?" And Catherine replied in the spirit of Simon Peter: "Thou knowest that I choose Thee. Thou knowest, for I have no other will but Thine, no other heart than Thine." Pleased with her reply, our Lord gave her St. Mary Magdalene for her mother.

On August 3, vigil of St. Dominic, in the church consecrated in his honor, Catherine encountered Fra Bartolomeo; he was seated on a bench and she knelt down beside him and began to talk. Suddenly her face lighted up and she began to gesticulate; in rapture she exclaimed: "Father, look at our Father Dominic! Don't you see him? Why I see him more clearly than I see you! And he resembles Our Saviour, with his oval face, handsome features, blond hair and beard. . . . He is so beautiful!" At that moment Stephen Benincasa approached — Stephen, her younger brother who as a little boy had distracted her in her first vision above the Church of St. Dominic. Once more Catherine turned to look at Stephen; and when she turned back to her vision the founder of her Order had disappeared. She burst into tears; and when Fra Bartolomeo returned three hours later he found her still uncomforted. She told him that St. Paul had appeared to her and reproved her for her momentary distraction.

On August 11 she had another singular vision: Our Lord permitted her to drink the blood from His wounded side; as she drank she tasted an ineffable sweetness that seemed to presage death. And she fell ill, so ill that on the Feast of the Assumption, a day she always looked forward to with a bit of anxiety, she was confined to her bed in the home of Alessia. Lying there, she reviewed in her mind the Liturgy of the day, so rich in grace, so replete with love of Mary, as it was being carried out in the new Cathedral[1] dedicated to God in honor of Mary's Assumption, with its naves of black and white marble arranged in horizontal lines, forming, as it were, a staircase toward heaven, reminiscent of the black and white Dominican habit, giving an impression of severity mingled with gaiety as they met the prayerful massed columns. "Ah, if I could only get a glimpse of the top of the campanile!" she was thinking. But high as it was, with its tower of black and white, the campanile, on the other side of the hill from the house of Alessia on the Via Casato, could not be seen from Catherine's bed. Nevertheless Catherine's wish was that of her Spouse: she had expressed a wish and He would grant it. In a twinkling there rose before her eyes the airy form of the campanile: she seemed to stand in the huge piazza before the Cathedral, the building of which had been interrupted both by the plague and by the tortuous affairs of the city. It seemed to Catherine that she climbed the steps to the Cathedral, entered the church, and assisted at the Pontifical Mass being celebrated by the Bishop in the midst of twinkling candles and clouds of incense.

On August 18, Feast of St. Agapetus,[2] she was able to leave her bed and go to church. One can imagine with what hunger she approached the altar to receive the Bread of angels! As the priest approached her with the Blessed Sacrament in his fingers and she pronounced the words, "Lord, I am not worthy that Thou shouldst enter my roof!" a voice replied: "But I am worthy that you should enter Me." Holy Communion became an exchange of souls, as if the soul of Catherine entered into her Lord and that of our Lord entered into her. So moved was she that, upon returning to her cell, she threw herself upon the wooden slab that served as her bed and remained there a long time stretched out as if dead. Some tertiaries were there in the room with her — among them Catherina di Ghetto, Alessia and, perhaps, also Lisa — and suddenly they saw her apparently lifeless body raised aloft. Later, again lying on her cot, Catherine awoke and began to speak upon the subject of wisdom with such evident feeling that the other sisters were moved to tears. Then Catherine began to pray for acquaintances, among them for her confessor. It so happened that at this moment this priest was wandering around in the Church of the Friars, distracted in his thoughts, when suddenly he experienced a lively desire to pray. Later on he learned from the Sisters that in that precise moment Catherine had asked for eternal life for him and for others; and in making this request she had extended her right hand, saying to her Spouse: "Promise me that Thou wilt grant it!" At these words she had experienced such acute pain that she cried out in agony: "May Christ our Lord be praised!" as she always did in moments of physical suffering.

Once when she had asked of Jesus a sign that her prayers were being heard, He made her hold out her hand, the palm of which He pierced with a nail. It was the beginning of the stigmata, later on made complete in 1375 in the chapel of St. Christian at Pisa.

There, after Holy Communion while she was in ecstasy, our Lord appeared to her on the cross and from His five wounds, five bloody rays pierced her hands, her feet, and her heart. The exquisite pain that she suffered was such that only through a continuing miracle could she endure it. However, our Lord granted her request that the stigmata would not be apparent to the eyes of the others.

Nevertheless, when Catherine returned from the chapel to the hospital where she was a patient she fainted. The sisters and the nuns, who now followed her as their teacher, were alarmed at these evidences of physical prostration for they were afraid of losing her; they adjured her not to approach her Spouse too closely and thus leave them orphans and they begged God leave her with them that they might learn from her heavenly wisdom. To Catherine's disappointment their prayer was answered and the pain of the stigmata ceased.

However, a short time after, when she returned to Siena she again felt pain from the wounds; but she herself begged of God to allow her to share in the sufferings of Christ. She had never refused the bitter chalice. For she had an interpretation all her own — worthy of "strong, perfect men," as she said — for the words of Jesus in the garden of Gethsemani: "Father, if thou art willing, remove this cup from me" (Lk. 22:42), the ordinary interpretation of which seemed to her worthy only of "weak men who are afraid of death." According to Catherine, our Lord, in that moment of desolation, asked His heavenly Father that He could now drink entirely the chalice of His desire to redeem men which He had been drinking all His life. That is to say, He did not ask that it be postponed but that it be hastened. "And although that chalice of desire seemed impossible to drink, nevertheless as a Son obedient in all things He added: 'Only as Thy will is, not as Mine,' . . . accepting thereby a delay in His desire." So that when our Lord asked: "Remove this cup from me," He referred, according to Catherine, not to the chalice of His Passion to come but to the Passion of the present and the past.

Raptures, ecstasies, visions, conversations — all were expressions of her one love: Jesus Christ. It was this love that, in a certain sense, freed her from her body and made her more than a mere human creature. It explains how she longed to die to be all with Him, how she desired nothing but His presence and His embrace. Her whole ascent from earthly things was aimed at being one with Him, so that, lost in Him, He would live in her. When she speaks of her Spouse, her words are afire, and in her ardor she saw Him above all in emanations of fire and blood. In those days of supreme union with her Spouse, she sought Him and loved Him in His Passion more than anything else, because in His Passion He had given the measure, without measure, of His love. And since she had determined to imitate Him, even to the point of identifying herself with Him, in His sufferings, choosing with Him and for Him opprobrium, physical pain, insults, scourging and death, so she attempted now to experience one by one the agonies of His Passion. Was not this the height of adoration? "Up, then, manfully, for the love of Christ crucified! Nail yourself to the cross with Christ crucified. Delight in the wounds of Christ crucified." This program, which she would later on suggest to the jurist, Francesco Montalcino, to mitigate the sufferings of his infirmity, she had long since proposed to herself. Hence the contrast between her and her disciples: they wanted her for herself; she wished only to die and be with Christ: . . . "desiring to depart and to be with Christ" (Phil. 1:23).

Catherine knew that the sufferings endured by Christ were the greatest possible, just as His love which inspired them was the greatest possible; both were incalculable. It was not nails which fastened Him to the cross — Catherine never tired recalling — but love. And now Catherine was to experience, within the limits possible to a creature, each and every suffering He endured; and to learn that His greatest torture was in the disjunction of the bones of His chest. This was her revelation on August 18 when she received the stigmata.

Pervaded by that fire and that blood, her love, like a burning flood, grew and extended to a point at which her heart seemed to burst and she seemed on the point of death. Indeed, to a group surrounding her she seemed already dead, and in the midst of their tears and sorrow someone went off to summon a priest. Fra Tommaso della Fonte and his confrere, Fra Tommaso di Antonio Caffarini, arrived at Catherine's bedside, dismayed and breathless, and began to recite the Church's prayers for the dying. Catherine remained cold and immobile. Other sisters, having heard the news, came up to the little room; two other friars also came, Fra Bartolomeo di Montuccio and the lay brother, Giovanni di Siena; the latter was so overcome by the scene that, suffering as he was from a heart condition, his weeping and grief caused the rupture of a blood vessel and severe hemorrhaging, that another death seemed probable. Everyone was in consternation. But Fra Tommaso della Fonte, Catherine's confessor and confidant, suggested to Brother Giovanni that he take hold of her hand and hold it to his chest. He did so and the hemorrhaging promptly ceased.

The fact was that Catherine was experiencing a mystical death, thus completing in her flesh the Passion of Christ. She felt that her soul was separated from her body and she contemplated the depths of divine life, something that she would always be powerless to express, because human memory could not reproduce it and human language could not express it. She contemplated two extremes: the glory of God and the punishment of sinners, above all the punishment of those who defile the sanctity of marriage.

Catherine had experienced, in her "beatific vision"[3] such rapture that had it not been for her desire to suffer even more, her return to natural life would have caused her a suffering truly unbearable. So she returned, her eyes opened, her blood flowed again through her veins and she regained consciousness, disappointed, resigned, her body as she remarked "torn to pieces" by her extraordinary experience.

Conversation with her Spouse was now more than ever intimate and loving, a continuous offering of herself to Him. "Thou, my sweet Love," she said to Him, "dost make and unmake, break and heal, this body of mine, housing a soul made to Thy image, eternal God. And I, miserable as I am, offer Thee again my life for Thy dear spouse, the Church. Any time that it pleases Thy goodness, take me out of my body and then put me back into it, each time with increasing suffering, so that I may see the reform of Holy Church. I beg you, eternal God, for the Church."

And God put the Church under her protection, gave her the task of making it over.

NOTES: *Chapter 10*

1. Begun early in the thirteenth century, completed during Catherine's lifetime, some years after the plague of 1348.
2. Pope and martyr (535–536).
3. The author here uses the term in a rather loose sense.

# III. Action

## 11. The Consolatrix of the Church

Espoused to Christ, having made His will her own, having received the marks of the nails and the spear and having died with Him, only the shell of Catherine Benincasa now remained: her spirit was Christ's. Within that frail body, perhaps the most spiritualized of all bodies, lived Christ, as if returned to this earth under the guise of a young woman.

She had come down from a temporary celestial vision; she had left her Lord in heaven, to find Him in His brothers upon earth. Up to then she had, with Mary, chosen the better part; now she also became Martha. Her Spouse had been God from all eternity; in time He became man. The Christian is another Christ if he unites in his person the human and the divine.

During her temporary death her spirit had seen the horrors of the damned, and Christ had told her: "Return to earth and point out to men their errors, their danger, their punishment." She might have hesitated, terrified at the thought of going back to earth, had He not added: "The salvation of many souls requires that you return; from now on you must not stay in your cell; indeed, you must leave Siena. . . . I shall always be with you; I shall guide and direct you;

you must teach the little people and the great, laymen and clerics and religious, for I shall give you wisdom and eloquence and no one will be able to resist you. I shall bring you into the presence of pontiffs of the Church and rulers of My people, to confound the proud, as is My custom by means of the weak." Receiving that mandate, her soul was reunited with her body.

As the legate of Christ, Catherine now considered herself in debt to all creatures; and she served them. But she served them to sanctify them. To accomplish this she assumed toward all, indiscriminately, an attitude of authority and of service, of love and of teaching. Jesus had loved all without distinction; she would love all without distinction. She made no distinction, therefore, between prelate and housewife, between pope and lay brothers, between friends and enemies; she saw only souls, for she thirsted for them. She warned the prior of Montoliveto, for example, that he might not make a distinction between legitimate children and those who were illegitimate, for the son of God had made no such distinction; He paid no attention to social position or to family trees, to lowborn or highborn, even, in a sense, to virtue or vice, but gave His love equally to every human creature.

She began her reform in Siena — the transformation of souls and the improvement of moral conduct. She achieved remarkable conversions, by insistent prayer and by personal interviews. In her desire to honor the Father, she saw in humanity a family that had to be freed from the slavery of Satan and she went about devouring (ac-according to her own expression) demons. There is the story, for instance, of two bandits, condemned to death, who were being transported to the "hill of the gallows," swearing, blaspheming, and cursing along the way (the street called "of the malcontents") while the executioners tormented them with hooks and pincers. Overcome by divine grace, through Catherine's prayers, on the threshold of the gallows they made their peace with God. Then there is the story of a young man in his early twenties, one Adrea di Naddino dei Bellanti, a boisterous, rowdy, and shameless unbeliever, who had, on one occasion, torn a crucifix from the wall and ground it under his feet. When he fell dangerously ill, he spurned the ministrations of his parish priest and then of Fra Tommaso della Fonte. At the latter's suggestion, Catherine, on the vigil of St. Lucy, October 12, placed the matter in the hands of our Lord. Through Catherine's prayers, Adrea was given the particular grace of a deathbed conversion and he died penitent on December 16, 1370.

Even more remarkable was the conversion of the entire family of Francesco dei Tolomei. One of the sons, Giacomo, was twice a murderer, and the daughters, Ghinoccia and Francesca, were complete worldlings. Through Catherine, Ghinoccia and Francesca were converted and became, along with their mother, Dominican Sisters of Penance; Giacomo became an honest and upright citizen, and a younger brother, Matteo, became a Dominican friar.

Another person, Nanni di Savini, was known among Sienese worldlings for his hauteur and his skill in sowing discord and fomenting quarrels among citizens, quarrels which resulted in more than one murder. How could this character possibly be converted — deceitful, mocking, typical product of a decaying civilization in which lethal, brute force made a shambles of human dignity and human liberty? Prelates and theologians had tried in vain. Anyone who mentioned the name of Catherine Benincasa was met with sneers. One day, however, Catherine ran into di Savini; she greeted him affably and engaged him in conversation, gradually drawing from his obdurate heart a subconscious desire for peace; freed of his incubus, he was suddenly overcome with joy, a joy such as he had not known for years. He burst into tears and told Catherine she had won. Falling upon his knees before her he exclaimed: "Holy virgin, I shall do as you say . . . take charge of my soul!" At her direction he first went to confession to Fra Raimondo, then to each one of his enemies to be reconciled with him. Now that Nanni Savini was no longer reckoned a dangerous enemy, the mayor of Siena had him arrested; there was talk of beheading him. Fra Raimondo betook himself to Catherine. "Sister, I'm afraid that the tender plant of conversion will be smothered and Nenni will end in desperation. . . . Protect him!" Catherine remained serene; she explained to the theologian that temporal punishment was a largesse in exchange for punishment eternal; however, He who had freed Nanni from hell would now free him from prison. And so it came about. Nanni was set free; in place of capital punishment he suffered the loss of much of his wealth; this, however, did not particularly displease Catherine, who knew full well how great an obstacle to holiness was riches. Later on Nanni gave the saint the castle of Belcaro, which she turned into a convent for her sisters giving it the name of Santa Maria degli Angeli.

Toward the end of 1370 Catherine's mother, Monna Lapa, fell sick. It was about two years since the death of her husband, whose loss had left a great void in her heart and had seriously crippled the family fortune. At the bedside of this parent, too, Catherine lavished her tenderest cares and her most pressing spiritual counsel, seeking to guide the spirit of the sick woman toward the liberty of paradise. Monna Lapa, however, would not listen; she had too many things to do; she had no time to die. The sick woman would not even go to confession. Instead she begged her daughter to obtain from God her recovery — if, as people said, she was a saint. And as Catherine prayed in church for her mother, Monna Lapa died without the sacraments. On that October day, Lisa, Catherine di Ghetto, and Agnola di Vannino were at the bedside, awaiting Catherine's return. One can imagine the latter's consternation at finding her mother dead. Impossible that our Lord would have inflicted upon her this tremendous disappointment! Her agonized invocations brought her mother back to life. Monna Lapa lived to be eighty-nine and became a Dominican Sister of Penance. The daughter had imparted to her mother an intensified spiritual life, turning her determinedly to God. And this was by no means her least miracle; for Monna Lapa had been as deeply absorbed in worldly affairs as her daughter was in those of heaven. The one was just as excited and quick in word and action as the other was calm and deliberate. One may say that Lapa had to undergo physical death in order that her daughter could re-call her to a new life, to become really the daughter of her daughter. Then for many years she was a real disciple of her daughter, and Catherine directed her with filial devotion, yet with firmness, so that like other disciples Monna Lapa learned to become a nothing (a "nonbeing"), to be patient instead of restive, to experience joy in tribulations.

People now came to Catherine from all around, to know her, to ask her questions, and to seek her help. And many there were who returned to their daily lives penitent and changed. This state of affairs came to the attention of the Pope, Gregory XI, who desiring to encourage this return of souls to God, by letters apostolic granted Fra Raimondo and two of his confreres the faculty of absolving, also in cases reserved to bishops, the sinners who at Catherine's urging went to them for confession. There were such crowds of penitents that many a day the priests could not leave their confessionals even for meals; while Catherine and her disciples, men and women, spent their days ministering to their needs.

Catherine regarded that penitent throng with the exultant joy of the spouse of Christ who had succeeded in snatching these souls from the clutches of Satan. This divine love with which He had loved men lent a compelling quality to her words and her smile. Then, too, news of the miracles she wrought, of the austerity of her life, of the works of charity she performed, all attracted to her an ever widening circle of persons who came to seek life from her: life of the spirit and health of body, to ask her counsel and her prayers, to obtain cures and material help. And she became all things to all men. Her followers were so enthusiastic that they usually fell upon their knees before her, to listen to her words. Those who could would kiss her hand or the hem of her tunic; failing in this they would kiss the stones of the pavement she trod. The puritanically minded, of course, murmured against such manifestations and were scandalized that she did not put an end to them. Catherine, however, as she later explained to her confessor, was unaware of these demonstrations.

Of the man in jail, Catherine would not stop to inquire about his guilt or innocence. He was a fellow creature; his soul should be free because it had been redeemed; he was capable by divine grace of being united and transformed in the consuming love of the Son of God; hence to be liberated from confinement here and servitude hereafter. Though incarcerated, he could make good use of his punishment, by coming to a true knowledge of himself, a process which would transform "the weariness and tribulation," by man's humility and God's mercy, into consolations.

These were her suggestions to all her followers, for all the vicissitudes of life: the jailed and the jailers, great and small, men and women. Even in prison there are not lacking temptations of the sort that she herself had experienced at those times when she was seized with mistrust and melancholy. She had learned to react against the danger not by abandoning her spiritual exercises but by increasing them.

Catherine's active apostolate by no means lessened her contemplative life; on the contrary, it drew upon contemplation as from the font and norm of action. During all that winter, which she passed in the home of Sister Alessia at the Saracini Palace, she had frequent ecstasies and visions. On Christmas night, as she knelt in silence before the crib, Mary gave her the Infant to hold for a moment; she fondled Him and kissed Him, whispering words of love. Later, at Mass, she saw an infant come out of the Host and from His bosom grew a vine laden with grapes which a pack of hounds, white and black, devoured.

This vision, Catherine believed, presaged the reform of the Church to be brought about by priests, especially the *Domini canes*, the hounds of the Lord, as she interpreted the name *Dominican*.

On New Year's Day, in church Catherine felt faint, whereupon the Blessed Virgin came to support her.

At Epiphany, though she was quite weak, she went to the church to make her obedience to Fra Tommaso. There she encountered our Lord again, this time surrounded by the saints she held most dear: John the Baptist, Dominic, Thomas Aquinas, Peter Martyr, Agnes, and Lucy. Jesus invested her with six shining tunics, presented by the saints one by one — to symbolize the principal virtues.

On the feast of the Conversion of St. Paul, January 25, she dragged herself to the church of St. Dominic, exhausted not so much by physical weakness as by spiritual depression; she seemed to be without faith, without hope, without love, all unworthy to appear before her Spouse. And, as a matter of fact, she did not go up to the chapel where the other Sisters were assembled but hid herself in a corner near the door, close to an unused altar. One of the Sisters caught a glimpse of her, however, and went over to her and led her over to the community to receive Holy Communion. The priest, though, when it came her turn, passed her by without giving her the Sacred Host. Then she assisted at two other Masses and the same thing happened twice more. Fra Bartolomeo Montucci, prior of the monastery had given orders not to give Catherine Holy Communion. The order was inspired by the prior's desire to avoid, on that day when crowds would be in church, any extraordinary manifestation of Catherine's mystical experiences. She, however, remained unperturbed. Convinced of her unworthiness she bowed to the will of God. But just when it seemed that she was to be denied Holy Communion, a bright light surrounded the altar and in the midst of it appeared a vision of the Blessed Trinity, the Father and Son seated upon thrones, and above them the Holy Spirit in the form of a dove. A hand of fire emerged from the vision, bearing a Host, and as a voice repeated the gospel narrative of the Eucharistic institution, the hand placed the Host upon the tongue of the virgin now in ecstasy.

On another occasion the Host alone left the altar and came to rest upon Catherine's lips.

During Lent she ceased to take any food at all and she remained completely fasting until the feast of the Ascension. She could swallow nothing and toward the end of her fast she was so weak she could not rise from her cot. However, on the morning of the feast she rose, vigorous and happy, to go along with Sister Alessia and the other Sisters to the church of St. Dominic. After Mass they all returned to the convent to breakfast upon a pot of peas sent over to them by the friars. Catherine ate with the rest, talked merrily with them and other disciples who dropped in, and even drank a glass of wine in the midst of the merry company.

## 12. Scribes and Pharisees

With the misdirected zeal of those who work to smother the Holy Spirit wherever He breathes, gossipers circulated insinuations about the saint, especially about her pretended abstinence from food. Strangely enough, during the years she had suffered from inability to take food, in order not to disturb well-meaning persons she had occasionally taken a few mouthfuls, though well knowing that she would have to vomit. On these occasions she would rise from table and whisper to the companions she most trusted: "It is time that this poor sinner satisfied justice."

Yet she did not react particularly to the gossip she provoked: she limited herself to observing that her critics really knew only the least of her faults; she asked only that they pray for her. One day, as she was lying ill on the cot in her cell, a religious, coming in with her confessor, loaded her with reproaches. With her arms folded across her breast she listened to the shower of abuse as she always did to her superiors, in silent humility. The priest was dumbfounded, and confessed that he was standing in the presence of a soul that was "pure gold."

The scandalmongers did not limit themselves, however, to the matter of Catherine's eating and drinking; the more imaginative went on to deride the relations between the nun and so many lay persons living in the world, between her and so many friars living in the cloister. The scandal mushroomed and soon became a pulpit theme. Fra Lazzarino da Pisa, eloquent Franciscan, professor of theology, rival of Fra Bartolomeo Dominici, set about confuting Catherine's teachings and scoffing at her works and those of her followers. His sermons were replete with phrenetic emphases and subtle distinctions. To buttress his arguments, he decided to visit the object of his attack. So on November 25, Catherine's feast day, in company with Fra Bartolomeo (who was convinced that Catherine would convert the Franciscan), he arrived at Catherine's house. The nun invited her visitors to be seated, but insisted upon standing before her inquisitor. The Franciscan hoped to catch her in error, particularly upon the point of private interpretation of Sacred Scripture, of which, among other heresies, he had accused her. She, however, defended herself by asking that he, a master of exegesis, enlighten her upon the matter.

At length, at the sound of the Angelus, Fra Lazzarino rose to go; Catherine accompanied him to the door and at the threshold she knelt to ask his blessing. He made a hurried sign of the cross and, quite distracted, returned forthwith to his monastery, convinced that he had dealt with a girl who, though pious enough, had little understanding. The following morning, he found himself without his customary youthful vigor for his daily tasks as priest and teacher; instead he was filled by a strange sadness which so increased in intensity that, unable longer to resist, he broke into tears; the more he strove against the depression, the stronger it became. As a logical man, he tried to analyze the feeling he had, sobs racked his body and more tears flowed. He felt quite unable to leave his cell and had to cancel his classroom lectures. At sunset when the Angelus sounded, he recalled the interview he had had the day before in Catherine's cell; he remembered the gracious young woman who had faced him, her black eyes flashing with an otherworldly light. He contrasted his own self-love, his many acts of vanity and pride, his constant searching for life's comforts, with the humility and dedication to God shown by that girl, living in the barest of cells.

Suddenly he realized the cause of his depression. His tears ceased; bitterness left him; his feeling of desolation subsided. Thereupon he determined to go again to Fontebranda, this time to confess his misery and to ask pardon. Early the next morning he knocked at Catherine's door; she herself opened it. Now it was the friar who knelt on the threshold. But she quickly knelt also, praying him to rise and enter the house. Catherine was simplicity itself, charming in a way she did not realize. She led him to her cell, where he sat beside her on the matting. It seemed in that moment that of all his learning there remained in his spirit only the words of the Gospel and the counsels of his father, Francis, the little poor man of God, and he suddenly exclaimed: "Until this moment I have known only the shell of Christianity; you possess its core!" So Catherine began to talk about Francis of Assisi and of the meaning of the rough habit, the rope with its three knots and the bare feet. In her words vibrated all the Franciscan ascetic; this, after all, was her life and preaching: to lose one's self in one's fellow man in order to arouse in him a divine awareness of his particular vocation. And since her visitor was a Franciscan she exhorted him to divest himself of all superfluous things and to give his money to the poor. She concluded: "Follow humbly in the footsteps of the crucified Christ and your Father Francis."

Then Catherine repeated a favorite theme of hers: that the religious order and the rule of life set up by every founder, once these be formally approved by the Church, are designed to sanctify the members of the order.[1] If this does not happen it is not the fault of the order or of the rule but rather the fault of the religious who do not follow the rule or who adulterate its spirit.

Fra Lazzarino, teacher himself, accepted the lesson as a docile pupil. Back in his room, filled with many books, with fine furniture and various conveniences, he gathered together everything not absolutely necessary, including many of his fine books and sold it all and distributed the money to the poor. He then became a living miracle of Catherine's influence upon souls. Leading a life of prayer and penance, he was happy to hear himself referred to, wherever he preached, as a disciple of Catherine.

The experience of Fra Lazzarino of Pisa was repeated with Fra Gabriele of Volterra, also a Franciscan, also a doctor of theology, also a famous preacher, who lived in his monastery in an apartment strangely elaborate for a son of the Little Poor Man of Assisi, with a comfortable bed and an elaborate library. He, too, preached against Catherine, charging her with heresy, especially because of what he considered her free interpretation of the Bible. Sharing his prejudices were Fra Giovanni Terzo of the Tanucci family, a pious Augustinian and an expert in theology. Together they decided one day to confront this ignorant girl and to confound her right before her deluded followers. They found her in the company of Malavolti, Pagliaresi, Piccolomini, Nicolo dei Mini, the Jesuate Father Tommaso Guelfaccio, Matteo Tolomei, Fra Tommaso della Fonte, and her Sisters Alessia, Cecca, and Lisa, and others. The two theologians proposed to Catherine some quite subtle questions on scriptural exegesis. She, however, was not concerned with theological casuistry; she disregarded their snares and, quite aware of the un-Franciscan life led by Fra Gabriele, she went after him directly: "How could you want to know something of the kingdom of God, you who live only for the world and long only to be esteemed and praised by men? With all your wisdom you are of little use to your fellow men and positively hurtful to yourself, because you seek the shell of Christ's teachings and not the kernel. For the love of Christ crucified, give up this life of yours!" Fra Gabriele, thus suddenly confronted with the Franciscan ideal, saw in a flash the horror of his own conduct; because he was fundamentally a good man, he took a bunch of keys from his cincture and gave them to Catherine and asked her: "Is there no one here who will go to my room, take away all it contains and make distribution to the poor?" There was indeed. The old Jesuate father, at a nod from Catherine, took the proffered keys and, along with a companion, betook himself to Fra Gabriele's room. From it they took all the furnishings and all the books, leaving only the Franciscan's breviary. A changed man, Fra Gabriele asked to be transferred to Florence; there he became the servant of his brethren at Santa Croce.[2]

As for the Augustinian, Giovanni Tanucci, likewise converted by

Catherine, he became one of her most humble and co-operative disciples. He later followed her to Avignon and to Rome, holding himself always available as a confessor for those whom she converted.

Now he retired to his monastery, in the Sienese quarter called Lecceto, where he observed the pristine rigor of the Augustinian rule. Nearby there were grottos inhabited by hermits. Among these, near the cloister called San Leonardo al Lago, in a cave furnished only with a few books, lived a hermit unusually learned and particularly dedicated to contemplation, the Englishman, William Flete, with whom, as it seems, Fra Giovanni had studied at Cambridge.[3] He introduced Flete to Catherine, who, much attracted to his ascetical life, made him one of her confessors while he, in turn, took her as his spiritual director. Catherine always had a difficult time in getting him away, even for a little while, from the solitude of his cell to meet some of the brethren, for the hermit longed only to spend each day in talking with God alone, in uninterrupted silence, even at the risk of failing in his duties to his monastery. He loved and venerated Catherine and would keep as relics bits of her vesture. At her death he was to write a long panegyric of her, but he never quite succeeded in overcoming his characteristic misanthropy when she invited him to come out of his solitude, like another St. Anthony, to lend a hand in rebuilding the Church, torn by schism.

These episodes point up one fact: that while most persons, through direct experience, now recognized in Catherine a saint of uncommon stature, a minority, lacking this direct knowledge, remained perplexed and kept on raising objections. There were in circulation, after all, many visionaries and many women frauds who were exploiting the ignorant and spreading teachings that were dangerous to sound doctrine and discipline. In Tuscany, for instance, the "fraticelli"[4] had been vigorously attacked a few years before by the hermit, Fra Giovanni delle Celle, because they had refused obedience to papal authority and in Florence were viciously attacking the "theologians," as they called the clergy of the city. In Umbria and elsewhere while they preached against a very real corruption of the clergy they went to such extremes as to provoke more scandal than usefulness, not to mention the fact that some of them propounded the wildest sort of interpretations of Sacred Scripture and proclaimed prophecies so subversive as to threaten the very foundations not only of religion but of the civil order as well. No great wonder, then, that in the popular mind the mantle of the virgin of Siena should be tarred with the same stain — After all did she not pretend to ecstasies, soul readings, prophecies, and wonder-workings?

Then, too, there remained the fact that Catherine was a holy woman; and holiness is a scandal to mediocre minds, to pharisees, and to anticlericals. Had she been a vulgar woman or even a bad woman, few if any would have bothered to notice; but she was a saint; she dared to practice heroic virtue while monks were lax and priests cynical and even episcopal Curias were venal. Hence, Catherine had continually to admonish her followers, such as Sister Daniella of Orvieto, to conform herself constantly to the Crucified, "in the midst of suffering, opprobrium, derision, insults, persecutions, not only from worldlings but also from the servants of God under the guise of virtue."

And "under the guise of virtue" they sought to suffocate Catherine's sanctity. At length the Pope himself, after Catherine had written him a letter, after having received the reports of his legates, and after who knows how many wild reports brought him from Italy[5] yielded to a suspicion and decided upon an investigation, which he entrusted, quite logically, to Fra Elia of Tolosa, master general of the Dominican Order, of which Catherine was a member.

So Catherine was asked to go to Florence to appear before a Chapter that was convened in June, 1374, at Santa Maria Novella[6] with the intervention of five hundred Dominicans, among whom were Fra Tommaso della Fonte and Fra Bartolomeo Dominici. Present also was the young theologian, Fra Raimondo of Capua, member of the family of Pier delle Vigne and already well known for his learning and his capacity for governing. He had heard of the virgin of Siena, it seems, from Fra Tommaso delle Fonte, at the monastery of Montepulciano, where Fra Raimondo had lived for about four years, until 1366, writing a biography of Agnes of Montepulciano, who lay buried there.[7] Acquaintance with the life of Agnes enabled Fra Raimondo better to understand Catherine of Siena; and since he was a good man, cultured and intelligent, he understood the sort of soul he was dealing with; hence just as he venerated the deceased Agnes he came to venerate the living Catherine; he became her follower and perhaps her most intimate confidant.

The careful examination of Catherine's teachings convinced the investigating friars of her orthodoxy and her virtue. Fra Elia himself appointed Fra Raimondo as her spiritual director, with the duty of aiding her in her apostolate for the pacification of Christianity and the reorganization of the Church.

NOTES:   *Chapter 12*

1. This truth, theologically expressed: Obiectum secundarium infallibilitatis est approbatio ordinum religiosorum quoad regulam in iudicio doctrinali (in quo Ecclesia speculative iudicat utrum certa regula sit via perfectionis an non) si fit in forma solemni (ultima et definitiva).
2. Built in 1294 by Arnolfo for the Franciscans.
3. In 1225 the Friars Minor had set up a house of studies at the University of Cambridge. The next year the Chancellor of the University was recognized by the Pope. Later on the Dominicans, the Carmelities, and the Augustinians had houses at Cambridge.
4. "Fraticelli" — the name given to a heretical sect which originated in the early fourteenth century. They gathered in isolated places, wore a habit like that of the Franciscans, lived upon alms, and preached many errors.
5. Gregory XI (Pierre Roger de Beaufort) was then residing in Avignon.
6. This church, Italian-Gothic in style, begun in 1279 and completed in 1357 with a Lombard campanile, was the work of Dominican friars.
7. St. Agnes of Montopulciano, a Dominican nun, canonized in 1726. Catherine had great veneration for her.

# 13. The Plague

Returning from Florence, Catherine found Siena in the grip of the plague. This epidemic of 1374 repeated the horrors of the pestilence of 1348. Again it was so violent that death claimed a third of Siena's people, among them Catherine's brother, Bartolomeo, and her sister, Lisa, as well as eight of Lapa's grandchildren. Another brother, Stefano, died of the plague at Rome.

Catherine could easily have fled from the horror; instead she chose to remain, with all her followers, to take care of the stricken, who had been pretty much deserted by their own people, offering personal service and all the material things she could lay hands upon. "The epidemic of our times" — sadly observed the author of the *Legenda Maior*, Fra Raimondo, echoing the words of Petrarch, himself its victim that year — "again and again devastates the world." Misfortune, epidemic, civil strife — the three-headed monster devoured the sons of men in the late middle ages.

Fra Raimondo, along with other friars, also remained to take care of the victims, usually making his headquarters the Misericordia Hospital, founded by the Sienese nobleman, Matteo Cenni di Fazio, who had been among the first of Catherine's followers, a man she loved and admired for his complete faithfulness to duty and the courage with which he disposed of his patrimony to serve the poor. Then one day Matteo, too, came down with the plague — stricken while at prayer in church — and was carried to a room in his hospital. He was colorless, speechless, wracked by spasms which convulsed his head and his groins, and burning with fever. "An able and conscientious doctor," named Senso, diagnosed it as the plague, in an advance stage, lethal; he promised, however, holding out but little hope, the therapeutic use of a certain extract of cinnamon. When the news reached Catherine, whose days and nights were now being spent assisting the sufferers, she threaded her way through the narrow filthy streets, holding a lantern and a flask of disinfectant. Reaching the hospital, she made straight for the room where the dying Matteo lay, and exclaimed: "Get up, sir, this is no time to be lying comfortably in bed!" This was not only her affectionate greeting to him; it was also her conviction that a Christian had no right to lose time during that emergency, that the proper place for the head of a hospital was certainly not in bed. Upon hearing Catherine's voice, Matteo literally leaped from his bed, fever and spasms gone. Exultingly he thanked her and thanked the Lord who, through her, had snatched him from what had seemed certain death.

News of the miracle raced through the corridors of the hospital, so that Catherine, in order to avoid group manifestations of enthusiasm and possibly of fanaticism, quietly and unobstrusively, at an opportune moment, disappeared from the scene. As the silent figure in white reached the door of the hospital she encountered Fra Raimondo who, as yet, had heard nothing of what had happened. They had told him that Matteo was dying and he was hurrying along, out of breath, to the bedside. Seeing Catheirne, excited as he was he reproached her: "Mother, will you permit a man so dear to us, so humble and so necessary, as Matteo, to die now?" "What words are these?" she replied, nettled, perhaps, and scolding him for his extraordinary greeting. "Am I then God that I should be able to free mortal men from death?" Fra Raimondo, too much preoccupied with the thought of his dying friend in a room upstairs to weigh his words, replied harshly: "You can use those words to others, but not to me, who knows your secrets and knows that whatever you ask of our Lord is always granted." Catherine bowed her head and smiled, and then looking him straight in the eye said laughingly: "Don't worry; this time he will not die." Fra Raimondo waited to hear no more; he took the stairs two by two to reach Matteo's room; there he found the patient happy and healthy, and on his feet. It seemed too good to be true, so they celebrated by having a meal together — not a meal for convalescents but for healthy, hungry men — talking no doubt about Catherine, through whom there was life and health and joy and escape from death!

For that matter Fra Raimondo himself was not spared by the plague. At Catherine's insistence, he had exposed himself to the risks entailed in continuous service of the afflicted, never sparing himself, bringing to the dying the last sacraments and the comforts of religion. He was almost the only priest in that crowded city, and he could easily have found an excuse to leave. One night, rising to recite the Divine Office, he felt pain in his groin and then discovered an inflammatory swelling of the lymphatic gland. Frightened, he decided not to get up but rather to prepare for death. He had seen so many cases like this that he did not try to delude himself. For then he began to notice all the other symptoms that were customary forerunners of death.

At daybreak, assisted by a companion, he dragged himself to Catherine's house. She, however, was absent, called across the city to care for plague sufferers. Unable to keep to his feet any longer, the friar stretched out upon a bed, while members of the household went forth in search of Catherine. Soon they found her, and when she came to the bedside of her trusted director and disciple she knelt and placed her hand upon his forehead and began to pray. It was a prayer so intense that she was rapt in ecstasy, "as on the other occasions," for a good half hour. Before Catherine regained her senses, Fra Raimondo after experiencing symptoms resembling lacerations of his body, realized that he was cured. Catherine, serene and at his service, had food brought to him and then fed him with her own fingers. Then "she told me to rest a while," says the friar, "and I quite willingly obeyed her." Later on he got up, stronger and more able than ever, and obeyed Catherine's order to get back to work, all the while rendering thanks to God.

In similar fashion, Fra Bartolomeo Dominici, stricken even more seriously, was cured.

Among other victims of the plague was a hermit, venerated by all Siena, named Santi, "a saint in fact as well as in name," who lived in a grotto on the outskirts. Hearing of his seizure, Catherine had him brought into the city to the Mercy Hospital; and with some other Sisters she went there to visit him. While the others busied themselves caring for him, she whispered in his ear: "Don't be afraid; even though you are very ill, this time you will not die." Then she was silent, while the friars and Sisters present, seeing the condition of the sick man, began to beseech her intervene with God. From her silence, however, they gathered that there was no longer any hope; and in fact the stricken man grew worse and worse. But Catherine whispered to him again: "Fear not — you will not die." Then began the death agony, accompanied by the labored death rattle, characteristic of plague victims, which was actually prolonged through several days. Those about his bed, who loved and venerated the hermit, continued to lament him. Again, Catherine whispered in the ear of the dying man, as if in a sigh: "I command you, in the name of our Lord Jesus Christ, not to die." "I command you. . . ." Who could resist an order given by this young woman in the name of God? Certainly not Santi, who knew her so well. And because he knew her, he obeyed: opening his eyes, he suddenly sat up in bed and asked for something to eat. He was cured. It was his lot, six years later, to assist, in tears, at her passing; and for years later he never stopped telling all who would listen how he had been not so much cured as brought back to life.

In the midst of the plague, she also saved one of her sisters who had slipped and fallen from a terrace at San Domenico, landing on stones a floor below. She was cut and bruised and had sustained several severe fractures, so that it seemed a miracle she had not been killed. Catherine touched the injured members one by one and healed them.

Finally, in autumn, the epidemic ran its course. The little community decided to take a short rest in the country. With Fra Raimondo and Sisters Alessia and Giovanna dei Pazzi, Catherine made a pilgrimage to Montepulciano to venerate St. Agnes. The Sienese maiden had found in the virgin of Montepulciano a kindred spirit: she looked forward to sharing with her a place in paradise. Among the nuns of Montepulciano were two of Catherine's nieces, daughters of her brother, Bartolo. So during the visit there were days of delight with them although there were also moments of physical exhaustion. Together with her nieces she paid a visit to nearby Val d'Orcia, where sun and verdure filled Catherine with such joy of living that momentarily she seemed to forget the cross.

During the plague, Catherine, an angel in white bringing health and hope to a world of the dying, had aroused much admiration even beyond the confines of Siena. From Pisa, for example, came urgent invitations from nuns, religious men, and lay persons for her to come and bring her message to that city. Catherine, although now twenty-eight years old, had never gone outside the region of Siena, and she hesitated to accept, especially since her followers were not of one mind on the matter. In those days, travel beyond the confines of the Sienese Republic, especially for an unmarried woman, seemed quite an adventure. She sought enlightenment from God and she was encouraged to go ahead; she placed the project under Fra Raimondo's direction and he bade her make the trip.

So she set out. She was accompanied by her confessor, by Fra Tommaso della Fonte, Fra Bartolomeo, and other friars, all prepared to hear the many confessions that inevitably were requested by those who saw Catherine and heard her.

They arrived in Pisa in February, 1375, and were guests of a disciple of Catherine, Gherardo dei Buonconti, whose brothers,

Tommaso and Francesco, were also her disciples. Gherardo introduced her to a young woman in her twenties who for eighteen months had been tormented with fever. For her medicine, Catherine prescribed a visit to confession, first to get rid of her interior infection; after the girl had confessed her sins, Catherine placed her hand upon her shoulder and healed her body; the fever vanished. Then there was the cure of a nun in San Domenico, Gemma, who suffered from severe angina. Throwing herself at Catherine's feet, she begged: "Mother, I shall die if you do not help me!" Catherine made the sign of the Cross over her and she was well.

At Pisa on April 1, *Laetare* Sunday[1] Catherine received the completion of the stigmata, and because of the accompanying spasms she had to be carried from the church of St. Catherine to her home, where she remained in danger of death until Passion Sunday. Her sufferings were not only physical but moral, the latter induced by evil-disposed persons who were quite displeased by her power of healing souls and bodies. Her circle of followers was constantly widening; her success aroused misunderstanding and envy. Was she a wonder-worker or charlatan? . . . Prophetess or heresiarch? Serious criticism was voiced also by really good people. Even Fra Raimondo echoing, perhaps, a common thought wondered about the habit her visitors had of kneeling before her and kissing her hands, assuming the posture shown in the painting of her follower, Vanni, now hanging in the church of San Domenico. . . . Why did she permit these actions of her devotees? Catherine, humble and smiling, bowed her head; of what importance was this ingenuous gesture of the people and what could it possibly mean to her, quite aware of her nothingness?

Others at Pisa ridiculed her for not eating; among these was a poet, a native of Siena, Bianco di Santi, a Jesuate, who expressed his perplexity in verse:

> Beware, beware I pray you
> Lest fame or word betray you.
>
> Men call you saint and holy.
> If God's Spirit lead you solely

Though the world praise and flatter
That will be little matter.

Should your faith meet disaster
Others will follow faster.[2]

When reluctantly Fra Raimondo had read to her this rhymed reproof, Catherine, saint that she was, not only was not offended but showed a kindly feeling toward the author; anyone who took the trouble to reprove her must love her; she wrote him a friendly letter, addressing him as "Most Reverend and most dear Father." According to her thinking, the honor of God and zeal for souls had made him fear that she was deceived by the demon. Hence if he feared, she trembled. She did not trust herself; she trusted only in God: "I trust only in the goodness of God; I have no confidence in myself." About the much-discussed matter of her eating, she recalled to him that she had tried in every way to take food and she had prayed God to let her follow the customary way of His creatures. But she had not succeeded; now she was asking him, Bianco di Santi, that he, too, would pray for this intention if it were for the honor of God and the good of her soul. However . . . one pays for love with love. Bianco had given her advice; now, in turn, Catherine, who wished to love him as herself, ventured to offer him one small counsel: "I ask that you be not quick to judge. . . ." And this was the gloss to Bianco's verse.

Then Bianco was joined by two other first-rate professionals. These two were the medical expert, Giovanni Gutalebraccia, and the noted lawyer, Count Pietro degli Albizzi da Vico: two luminaries of the intellectual world, who brought to the discussion the prestige of their scholastic degrees and, still more, of their commanding personalities. To weaken Catherine's position at the very outset, they asked her if God when speaking had a mouth and lips, the necessary organs of speech. The question was like certain subtle sophisms proposed by the Pharisees to Jesus. It was, however, if possible, even more clumsily stupid. For Catherine simply replied that it mattered

Statue of the Saint in the lower chapel of the family home in Siena

The Saint cutting off her hair to dedicate herself to the religious life — from a painting in the family home

Her father finding the Saint at prayer — from a painting in the family home

The mystical betrothal—from a painting in the family home

The Saint giving clothing to Jesus, who appears to her in the guise of a pilgrim — from a painting in the family home

The miracle of the woman possessed —
Church of St. Dominic, Chapel of St.
Catherine, Siena

The Saint receiving the crown of thorns
from Jesus — from a painting in the family
home

The Saint falling unconscious after receiving the stigmata — Church of St. Dominic, Siena

The Saint receiving the Infant Jesus from the Blessed Virgin — from a painting in the family home

Entrance to the family home of the Saint, Siena

Courtyard of the family home, Siena

The healing of Matteo Venni — from a painting in the lower chapel of the family home

An angel bringing the Saint Holy Communion — Church of Dominic, Siena

Levitation — from a painting in the family home

Tomb of the Saint beneath the high altar of the church of S. Maria sopra Minerva, Rome

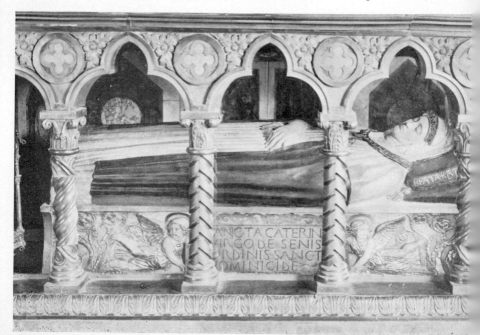

little whether God had vocal apparatus; all that mattered to her was to love Jesus and to believe in Him. How were the savants to reply to this disarming answer? The two pundits beat an ignominious retreat, to meditate upon the wisdom of this young woman; and thus meditating, they began to understand the difference between substance and appearance; and they both ended by believing in her. Indeed, Pietro degli Albizzi asked her to act as sponsor for a child that his wife was about to have.

The impression Catherine left at Pisa was so profound that the following year another invitation came to her, this time signed by the Governor of the Pisan Republic himself, Piero Gambacorti. The invitation shows further the close friendship established between Catherine and the Gambacorti family, one of whose daughters, Tora, inspired by Catherine, was to become a nun, taking the name of Chiara, and was to die in the odor of sanctity.[3]

During this second stay in Pisa, Catherine was busy principally with the Crusade.[4]

Also during her stay in that busy Republic, she visited the more important religious centers, from the famous Camposanto[5] to the Carthusian monastery of Valle Graziosa; from Calci[6] all the way over to Gorgona[7] to talk with the Carthusian monks there, at the behest of their prior, Bartolomeo Serafini. She was accompanied on these trips by friars and nuns, and as she spoke to the white-robed monks of Gorgona, under the inspiration of the Holy Spirit she revivified in them the ideal of monasticism. One young monk who was on the point not only of leaving the cloister but of committing suicide, in a crisis of desolation, was so moved by Catherine's words that he returned to the complete ideal of Chartreuse and again found complete joy in the companionship of his brethren.

The prior was so pleased with the results achieved by those inspired words in her talks to his monks, touching each heart in its inmost needs, that he confessed to Fra Raimondo that every monk had been reformed in precisely the point where he needed reforming. At his insistence Catherine left her mantle with the community as a reminder of her visit.

NOTES:  *Chapter 14*

1. Fourth Sunday in Lent.
2. This verse is by Sister M. Madeleva, C.S.C., to whom grateful acknowledgment is made. The Italian runs:

> Guarda, guarda, guarda
> che non diventi bugiarda
> . . . . . . . . . . . . . . . . . . . . . . .
> La tua fama attorno e gita.
> santa se' gia nominata!
> Se lo Spirito ti mena
> non cercar loda terrena.
> Se tu cadi, molta gente
> caderebbe discredente.

3. She died April 17, 1419, at the age of fifty-seven. Pope Pius VIII raised her to the altar.
4. Pope Gregory XI had ordered the Crusade and entrusted its propaganda to Catherine. Pisa, then a maritime center, was a good spot for her work.
5. Cemetery. The monumental burial place, near the Cathedral, formed of four vast corridors, called "the most beautiful artistic cemetery in the world." It dates from 1278.
6. A suburb of Pisa, on the right bank of the Arno. It has a beautiful church dating from the eleventh century.
7. A sterile island 21½ miles from Leghorn, inhabited mostly by fishermen.

## 15. Political Action

Among the prophecies committed to writing by the hermit, Fra Guglielmo (William Flete) in his cave of San Leonardo al Lago, at Lecceto, one has come down to us in which he foresaw the loss of his native England to the Church of Rome. It is quite probable that he, a keen observer of current affairs and a remarkably learned man, possessing an extraordinary religious sensibility, had discovered in the monarchies of western Europe that same tendency to override the Church that had prevailed in eastern Europe, following the example of Constantinople: a tendency favored not only by a growing paganism which brought men's consciences under political authority and thus aggrandized the state, but also by a growing exaggerated nationalism which threatened to tear to pieces the universality of the Church. Nearby France, ruled by a most powerful dynasty, presented a sad example. The Pope then resided at Avignon instead of at Rome, attracted and favored by the French kings who were so eager to use the papacy as a tool of empire and reduce the Pope to a sort of royal chaplain.

The papal exile in Avignon — the Babylonian captivity as Church historians bewailed it — followed the insult of Anagni where the

minions of the French king, Philip the Fair, laid hold of and
shamefully treated the seventy-year-old Pope Boniface VIII. The
millenary understanding between religion and politics had been
lacerated. The King of France was the only Catholic sovereign not
subject to the Emperor; he wished not to be subject to the Pope
either. In fact he was not, even then. The papal residence at Avignon signified that the Pope was at the mercy of the Capetian
dynasty[1] in whose realm he was given hospitality and royally im-
prisoned.

While men worked out a theory[2] by which state sovereignty was
not subject to but above all law, whether human or divine, there
began to appear the caesaro-papistic figure of a king endowed with
papal prerogatives, depending directly upon God, as His minister,
free of every ecclesiastical sanction; there evolved, in other words,
an autonomy and a set of prerogatives that signified the dominance
of the temporal order over the spiritual and favored the royal
cupidity to limit and even to take possession of the goods of the
Church.

Philip the Fair, in order to resist the Papacy at Rome and to
dominate the clergy in France, had prepared the framework of what
was to become the "French Church" and had caused an assembly
of nobles and ecclesiastics, convoked in 1302 in the Cathedral of
Notre Dame, to proclaim the absolute independence of the monarch
from the Church. When Pope Boniface VIII resisted, a royal minister, William of Nogaret, along with his followers, had assaulted him
at Anagni and had actually struck the aged pontiff. The Pope died
of a broken heart; and his successors, beginning with Clement V,
transferred their residence to Avignon to signify, even externally,
their complete subjection to the Capetian dynasty. Laicism had
achieved its first great victory over ecclesiastical power: the temporal
power had vanquished the forces of the spirit.

Even when poets, such as Dante and Petrarch, fascinated by the
universality of Rome, pleaded for the return of the Holy See to
the banks of the Tiber, they did so from motives that were not
less political than spiritual. On the other hand, when souls close
to God, like Brigid of Sweden and Catherine of Siena, attempted

to bring back the Papacy to its rightful residence, they did so not only to re-establish the apostolic order (the Pope is the Bishop of Rome and he should reside in his episcopal see, where he is the successor of St. Peter, the first Pope), but also to liberate the Vicar of Christ — and hence spiritual autonomy — from the most encroaching monarchs of the time, as well as to restore to Italy, and above all, to Rome, a bit of order. For, with the Pontiff away from Rome, the capital of Christendom had fallen prey to the noble families of Latium, had become the target of factions and quarrels and plunderings of adventurers and brigands, so that the few pilgrims who still ventured the wearisome and dangerous trip to venerate the tombs of the Apostles frequently fell into the hands of ruffians or were robbed and even murdered by soldiers of fortune.

The Pope was represented in Italy and carried on his duties through Cardinals who were his legates or diplomats or even men of arms! And that mixture of the sacred and the profane, whether in the Pope himself or in his representatives was hardly calculated to conserve the purity of religious sentiments in the peoples of Christendom. Anticlericalism, of which the Decameron of Boccaccio was a pungent expression, was due, as was the decadence of morality among ecclesiastics, to this sad juxtaposition of the sword and the crozier. When Innocent VI, in 1354, entrusted to Cardinal Gil de Albornoz[3] the task of restoring papal authority in the states of the Church, he was placing his cause in the hands of a band of mercenary troops and relying for success upon military alliances and battles, inflicting great cruelty upon the helpless population, yet daring to conduct the campaign under the name of a crusade. Thus a "crusade" was proclaimed by Pope Urban V in 1363, against Bernabò Visconti[4] and produced the anomaly of troops and equipment, recruited for use against Mussulmans, being hurled against a Christian prince, bestial though he was.

Through the victories of his legate, Urban V could hear the cries emanating from every part of Christendom to leave Avignon and return to Rome. So at length return he did, amidst the rejoicing of the Romans, in October, 1367. The next year Charles IV came to Rome to be crowned emperor of the Holy Roman Empire. Yet in 1370 the Pope was persuaded to return to his peaceful retreat on the Rhone and set out again for Avignon, to the anguish of St. Bridget who, after making a pligrimage to the various sanctuaries of Italy, returned to Rome to live among her nuns and to die there three years later (1373) without ceasing to send appeals to the Pontiff to come back to his See.

The following year there descended upon Italy, at the head of mercenary troops another Cardinal, the Frenchman Pierre d'Estaing, Bishop of Ostia, legate of the new Pope, Gregory XI. Gregory, elected in 1370, desired the reform of the Church and the renewal of the Crusade. However, he felt constrained to renew the war against Bernabò Visconti, using for the purpose an army of adventurers headed by the famous English soldier, John Hawkwood, whom the Italians called "Acuto." In view of the fact that the Bishop of Ostia now represented the Pope, Catherine boldly wrote to him. Her letter was written in a tone which, while completely respectful, was quite unhesitating, for, in her, charity was now one with truth. Playing upon the word "legate" (from the Latin, *ligare*, to bind) she told the prelate that she wished him to be "bound in the bond of charity. . . . Charity is that sweet and holy bond that binds the soul to its Creator; it binds God to man and man to God. . . . It gives peace and takes away war." For her the Christian cannot but seek the love of God and the good of neighbor. "Now in this mind and in this love I ask that you go forward . . . with manly heart." The gentle girl gave a commandment of power to the man of arms; only she meant a spiritual power, superior to military successes; she meant Christian charity. In substance she demanded of the papal legate personal holiness of life, even as a condition of the fulfillment of his legation. And she concluded her letter: "Be solicitous and not negligent; from this I shall know if you are really a legate and if you really want to bring about the triumph of the Cross." This last thought was always uppermost in her mind; she longed for the cessation of that fury of arms, that fever of war, so that the "crusade" would be directed not so much against the infidels as for the reunion of Christians.

Another prelate who "protected" the interests of the Church in Italy more by means of arms and intrigues than with faith and morals was the Abbot of Marmoutiers, Gerard du Puy, who roamed the peninsula setting the fire of discord among the powerful adversaries of the Holy See. This man, who at one time had made himself the intermediary between St. Bridget and Gregory XI, his uncle, had not sought the same role in Catherine's case. Evidently he had heard about her; and he suspected that the prophetic spirit of the Swedish seer was now continuing in the Sienese girl. So he wrote her a letter. Catherine's reply has been preserved for us. As usual, she did not regard him as the high dignitary (she had no need of a protector, having chosen for her inheritance the shame of the Crucified) but rather a soul to be straightened out. This soul, when once set right, would also rectify diplomacy. So she faced up at once to concrete particulars: the nepotism of the Pope (of which the Abbot himself was a product), and his weakness in governing the Church — two grave abuses to be corrected. At the same time she insisted that three sources of corruption be eliminated: immorality, avarice, and pride, which were rampant even in the government of the Church, where there were prelates who, in Catherine's words, "were concerned with nothing but pleasures, position, and wealth. . . . (They) are like wolves; they are trafficking in things divine." A radical reform was called for: "to repair the damages, it is necessary to begin with the very foundations."

She asked for a revolution: a radical Christian revolution continually working in holiness of consciences and of institutions. Catherine envisioned a veritable hurricane which would sweep away all the filth in high places; and to this undertaking she called upon the Pope and the Abbot, working together manfully, to cast out "the wolves, the devils incarnate in pastors who cared for nothing but to revel in their lovely palaces and upon their fine horses." In her biting words sounds the contempt of Dante: "Alas, that which Christ acquired on the Cross is being squandered on prostitutes!"

Without realizing it, Catherine was pointing to her own life in her reproofs: her chastity, her poverty, her humility. . . . How to repair that havoc? First of all, by removing unworthy pastors; then, by naming worthy ones, without succumbing to simoniacal influences, but attending only to the virtues of each candidate.

"Gregory XI," writes Jorgensen,[5] a biographer of Catherine, at this point, "undoubtedly received Catherine's message, but he gave no indication of following her advice. Instead, on December 21, 1375, he created nine new cardinals (among whom was Gerard du Puy himself), all lacking the qualities which Catherine had demanded. The best of them was the Spaniard, Pedro di Luna, the future antipope Benedict XIII."

Catherine had good reason, therefore, to foresee a future still more ruinous for the Church of Christ. The elevation of the Abbot of Marmoutiers to the purple rewarded his intrigues to sow dissensions in Italy between princes and communes. On his part, the ambitious and villainous Bernabò Visconti threw all of his resources into the battle against the papal party, creating new enemies of the Pope on all sides but paying particular attention to Florence and Siena. The Pope excommunicated Bernabò and Galeazzo Visconti[6] and raised up a fitting successor to du Puy in the person of the Frenchman, Guillaume du Noellët who, descending again upon Italy, devoted himself anew to snares and traps, conspiracies and crimes, factions and internecine struggles, all intensified by crimes of simony and corruption of priests and monks. Catherine, though a fragile creature, did not become discouraged and was not content with weeping; she reacted energetically.

She would sue the forces of the Holy Spirit against the onslaught of evil spirits. An atmosphere of terror hung over Tuscany and, indeed, over all Italy; but Catherine feared neither the poison nor the dagger of that Bernabò Visconti, who had forced the papal legates literally to eat the parchment upon which his excommunication had been written.

For that matter, Bernabò himself had asked Catherine's prayers for divine guidance, in a letter delivered to her by his representative at Siena together with a personal message from his wanton wife, Beatrice della Scala. Catherine replied in characteristic fashion: that is, she took exactly the opposite point of view from theirs and tried to direct their feverish bellicosity against the flesh and the devil and to turn their desire for glory into a desire for things eternal. She tried, in short, to interest them in a spiritual nobility, involving war against passions, reserving the use of arms for a true Crusade. True, she said, for such reversal of conduct the despot of Milan would need first of all the pardon of his sins, through the grace of Christ which the Church dispenses in the sacraments. But one disobedient to the Pope may not receive these graces. Hence, the Pope, the only Vicar of Christ upon earth, must be obeyed, even though he be an evil man, even though he be the devil incarnate. An insurrection against him, even though made under the pretext and the illusion of war against bad shepherds, cannot be justified in the eyes of God.

In this concept Catherine shows clearly her grasp of the doctrine of the Mystical Body of Christ: the decadence of some members, even of the visible head, is to be remedied not by lacerating the Body but by developing holiness — wholeness — in its members. Because she herself was holy, she would reform the Church by becoming more holy; because Visconti was a sinner, he would deform the Church by giving way to his passions.

She wrote another letter, also respectful but firm, as from a mother to a daughter, to Visconti's wife, and it stirred up in Milan the desire to have the Sienese girl visit that city. A letter written to Catherine in Latin about that time (May 30, 1375) by Elizabeth of Bavaria, daughter-in-law of the Visconti, bears witness to the reputation that Catherine enjoyed among the Milanese for her "immaculate chastity," her "purity of life," not merely according to human nature but by the divine grace so luminously apparent in her; it expresses the joy experienced in Milan at her promise to visit that city. Evidently Catherine had determined to confront Visconti face to face in order to induce him to make peace with the Pope and to join forces in a crusade against the Turks. That she did not make the trip was probably due to the fact that on June 4 an armistice was signed between the papal legate and Visconti, a direct result of which was that Giovanni Acuto and his lawless bands turned upon Tuscany, whose cities such as Siena and

Pisa and Florence were already financially exhausted in their efforts to resist or defeat or buy off the hirelings. But again Florence, in order to free her territory from the brigands — who went around plundering, burning, outraging, and who, when they did not kill, took prisoners both women and men — had to pay 130,000 gold florins.[7] And Pisa, Acuto's next victim, had to pay him 30,500 florins.

During the thirteen days while Acuto had been ravaging the Pisan countryside, Catherine boldly sent him a letter, delivered by Fra Raimondo and another Dominican. In her letter Catherine addressed him as "very dear brother," but she also characterized him as a minion of the devil and, to soften the title somewhat, she invited him to change his band of adventurers into "a company of Christ," thus to reply to the invitation of the Holy Father. Fra Raimondo explained to Acuto the thought of Catherine and the papal bull urging a crusade and, in view of the fact that those mercenaries had already promised ten years before to depart for the Holy Land, he obtained a renewal of the promise.

This time they might have kept their promise but on the 24th of that very month the truce expired between the Pope and Visconti, who, now allied with the Florentines, began to form an antipapal league among the Tuscan republics. In an effort to keep Lucca from joining this league, the Pope sent Catherine to talk to the elders of that city, who, accustomed as they were to making a game of politics, made promises without any intention of keeping them.

Catherine did not hesitate to rebuke those heads of state who were willing to go through the motions of siding with the Pope; however, with equal candor she declared to the Pope himself that the rebellion against him was due principally to the actions of the evil pastors and rectors sent by him into Italy.

She wished to eliminate the effects but also, and before all else, the cause of disorder — which was moral. With this in mind, she exercised her apostolate among the people as well as among the leaders. And among the people this apostolate was more fruitful. With the assistance of her nuns in Lucca, she induced innumerable souls to change their way of life, and her priest-followers, Fathers Caffarini, Dominici, and Fra Tommaso della Fonte, had to spend long hours hearing confessions. Naturally at Lucca, as elsewhere, there was not lacking the trickery of the scribes and pharisees: it was a priest who, called one day to bring her Holy Communion, actually dared to bring an unconsecrated host. When Catherine showed no sign of reverence or adoration, he began to reprove her. But she interrupted him: "Are you not ashamed, Father, to bring me common bread and cause me to commit an act of idolatry?" It is likely that the priest was indeed ashamed of himself; there is no record. However, there have come down to us a number of documents which show the enormous impression which Catherine made — letters which she wrote in answer to various civic personalities, among them the elders of the city and various ladies.

Influenced by the errors and the crimes committed by the French ecclesiastics and functionaries, incapable of understanding the Italian mentality, little by little not only Siena, Urbino, Todi, and Forlì, but more than eighty other cities of central Italy revolted against the Pope; so that the Vicar of Christ upon earth was the object of fierce anticlericalism among whole populations. Returning to Pisa, Catherine found the district seething; to Fra Raimondo and Fra Pietro da Velletri, who arrived there on December 2 to tell her of their consternation at the state of affairs, she said, as if prophesying: "Don't begin your tale of woe at once, because you will have even more cause for weeping. What you now see will seem like milk and honey compared with what is to come." Seeing that Fra Raimondo could not imagine the apostasy getting even worse, she added: "Now it is only lay persons; soon it will also be ecclesiastics." She had foretold the great schism.

She returned to Siena for Christmas.

NOTES: Chapter 15

1. The third dynasty of French kings, derived from its first ruler, Hugh Capet, through fourteen kings in direct line.

2. Introduced doctrinally by Marsilius of Padua (Marsiglio dei Mainardini) and John of Jandun in their work, Defensor Pacis, the totalitarian system, variously known as Gallicanism, Josephinism, and Jurisdictionalism, all included under the term, regalist, propounded these theses, condemned by Pope John XXII on October 23, 1324:

"All temporalities of the Church are subject to the emperor, who may deal with them as his own."

"The emperor may correct the pope, install him, depose him, and punish him."

"The whole church has no power to punish any man except by consent of the emperor."

3. Gil Alvarez Carillo de Albornoz, Spanish soldier and prelate.
4. The Visconti were a powerful Lombard family, of the Ghibelline faction, furnishing ruling dukes.
5. Johannes Jorgensen, Danish poet, journalist, and novelist, a convert to the Church.
6. Galeazzo II, brother of Bernabò. They were nephews of Galeazzo I and ruled jointly.
7. The gold florin weighed about 54 grains and was first minted at Florence in 1252.

# 16. Catherine's Followers

From the time she was a mere child not a few of Catherine's contemporaries, attracted to her both naturally and supernaturally, had begun to follow Catherine and to imitate her. The love that radiated from her added a sort of divine vividness to her natural attractions: black eyes, smiling lips, graceful body, vivacious reactions. So, gathering about her Christocentric ideal those souls who longed to give themselves to God, she early became their teacher. And as such she continued until the very end, always without any harshness, always familiarly at ease, always with an authority at once intimate and mysterious, so that, even while she was yet a mere girl, her disciples called her "Mother," frequently adding to the title such words as sweet, venerable, saint, revered, dear, joyous, lovely. And she from the first called them her children, even though in age and in dignity they were often her superiors. She accepted her role as mother, she concerned herself about everyone of her followers every moment of their existence and she looked upon them even from afar with a mother's love. At her home, when they were around her, she busied herself about household chores: in preparing meals, in looking after their clothes, in caring for their health, having regard for each as divine love inspired her and thus rendering everyone better and happier.

Even during the period when she had lived cloistered in her

cell, by her penances and her piety she had attracted the admiration and devotion of her sisters in religion and her friends: Alessia, Lisa, Francesca, the two Catherines, and later on Giovanna Manetti, and still later her own mother, Lapa.

Catherine lived, especially during the entire period of her public action, always surrounded, as if borne up and integrated, by her followers, formed in her likeness and in a certain sense become one with her. And from her earliest girlhood, according to the most inflexible Christian practice, she always sought the counsel and the instruction of priests, generally Dominicans, who, however, one by one, became her disciples. In these men we can measure the power of her attraction and the rarity of her wisdom: these teachers and directors of souls became her disciples, obeyed her, followed her. It is moving to note with what reverence the master general of the Dominicans, her confessor, Blessed Raimondo, a learned and holy soul, a diplomat and man of extraordinary experience, who had served as papal legate to communes and to kings and to the emperor and who had refused both the miter and the purple, calls, after the Saint's death, her whom he had obeyed as a mother and teacher, an angel "come on earth to work miracles."

And Catherine accepted the deference of those great names, for she saw Jesus Christ in them; she loved them in God and for God.

After the nuns and the friars came laymen and laywomen, married and single, such as Matteo di Cenni Fazi and Francesco di Lanco, who, when they came upon Catherine at her prayers, wished to be her disciples; and, later on, the young poet, Neri di Landoccio de' Pagliaresi, who asked the unlettered girl to receive him as her "son," and also presented to her Gabriele di Davino of the Piccolomini family and Francesco Malavolti, rich, elegant but volatile, and others. Still more wealthy worldlings, too, companions of Malavolti, the young Neri di Guccio degli Ugurghieri and Niccolò di Bindo Ghelli were her conquests: they had thought to amuse themselves at her expense, but they, along with many other rich and frivolous men of the world ended by agreeing with the fun-loving Malavolti: "There's no use; no one can escape the charm of this holy virgin!"

Her followers who dwelt at a distance from her never tired of talking about their "mother"; their veneration, however, did not, it seems, permit them to write to her, although she never held herself aloof. She was always joyful among her followers, and she approached them with a luminous purity shining through her black eyes, suggesting the presence of God. For precisely this reason, upon approaching her they were impelled to kneel before her and kiss the hem of her black mantle. Although they did not write directly to her, they did write to one another about her with reverence and purity of motive.

"Our sweet mother. . . . More I shall not say now except to ask you to embrace her for me. . . . I confess that our most amiable mother is really a mother to us." The good Maconi knew no better way to express his sentiments: we can see that Catherine means everything to him on earth and he expects her to be his gate to Paradise. He confesses that he cannot wait to throw himself at the feet of "my most beloved mother," "our venerable, sweet and gay mother."

The puritans grumbled at all this; the pharisees cried out at the scandal; but Catherine was too much occupied with contemplating the souls of her followers, loving beauty and hating evil. Her followers were called *caterinati*, creatures of Catherine, children of Catherine; the "beautiful brigade," "our group," as Catherine herself called them, setting them thus in contrast with the "worldly brigade."[1] Some, like Ambrogio Voliti, even called themselves by the masculine form of Catherine's name *Caterino*, so keenly did they desire to identify themselves with her. Stefano Maconi was a contemporary of Pagliaresi and, like him, young, elegant, and noble. Approaching her at first only with the idea of seeking her good offices in bringing peace between his own family and that of the Tolomei, he was at once entranced with her courtesy and happiness and abruptly changed his way of life to follow her inseparably as her secretary. Although he was about her own age, he called her "mother" and she called him "son."

Maconi also became one of the amanuenses who made it his business to transcribe the sayings of their "mother." Like the others, on more than one occasion, he committed to writing his sentiments of veneration and love for her: a love that was the poetry and the strength of their life, because they were all one in their life of prayer.

Similar sentiments were nourished and expressed by young and old, nuns and married women, rich and poor, ecclesiastics and laymen, by Catherine's relatives and by those unknown to her, a certain sign of the universality of that love which was a projection of divine love itself: the particular characteristic of that communion of saints. "Where two or three are assembled in my name, there I am in the midst of them" (Mt. 18:20). Jesus had promised; and our Lord was in the midst of them through Catherine who united them all in Him.

Thus they accomplished among themselves that participation of joys and of merits — of life — which is the communion of souls in the Mystical Body; and thus as a matter of fact they constituted an organism in which circulated the blood of the bleeding Lamb, for which the mother never ceased to stimulate their thirst. Almost like a mother of the Church, in them she begot the Church, she made them a living Church. With this in mind she fostered among them that mutual exchange of love which bound them to Jesus in a "union" stronger than could be devised among all the demons of hell: the "union of divine charity," the effect of an intense interior life, founded upon knowledge of oneself. "I desire and I command you that you be subject to one another, that you bear each other's weakness. . . . Hence, this is my wish for you, my dearest children: love one another, love one another all together." In this vein she wrote to a Fra Raimondo, to the Augustinian Giovanni Tanucci, and to their companions who were then at Avignon. From afar she accompanied them in charity, she formed them and sanctified them in truth, with sure authority, in the footsteps of Jesus, who had left His disciples precisely this heritage: "peace and unity and that they should love one another."

There was no resisting her holiness: she loved souls; she loved each one individually, as each person should be loved in a particular sense, even to the point of contemplating them in a sort of ecstasy, because upon each soul she stamped the image of the Creator and each one became a temple of God. She became one with each of them, identifying herself with their needs, their sufferings and their joys, and taking upon herself, before the tribunal of God, the responsibility and the burden of each one's conduct. She felt that this was her obligation and in this way she bound each soul to herself and herself to each soul, interposing herself, as Christ had done, as a victim of expiation before the justice of the Father. She did this as her first act immediately upon encountering a soul, immediately dedicating herself to assume his faults and to bear his punishment.

So, one by one she guided them and corrected them, enabled by her interior vision to see their hidden defects, just as walls and mountains could not hide from her their shortcomings. Before her there was no pretending: either one was in the state of grace or he hurried off to confession.

Haughty youths, wealthy patricians whom she won over to God turned their backs upon comforts and frivolities to follow her and to be enrolled in the magic circle of her love. They could perhaps tear themselves away for a day, or even for a year, but they always came back. For love makes two into one; and Catherine, making followers, made them one with her, for in their souls live the One Jesus Christ. Then when far away, she wrote to the mother of Stefano Maconi: "Do not be disturbed that I have kept your Stefano so long; I have taken good care of him, since by love and affection I have become one with him; I have taken your affairs as my own. . . . You, his mother, have given him birth once; now I wish to give birth to him and to your whole family in tears and suffering, to continue my desires and my prayers for your eternal salvation."

This was supernatural motherhood; it regenerated sons to supernatural life, taking a family and developing it as a prolongation and amplification of her own person or, rather, as an integral part of herself. She prayed for them, convinced that it was God's will that she should love them with a particular love; and she drew comfort from their virtue, confident of increasing them for the honor of

God. She formed them one by one after her own characteristic ideal of perfection: which was that of a rational illumination through which, recognizing oneself in God, he should die to himself and live completely dedicated to God and to his brethren, never judging, never being scandalized, never murmuring. It would have been easy during those times to be scandalized at the behavior of many members of the clergy and the laity; Catherine, however, would have them leave judgment to God, who permitted decadence and ruin and allowed tests and shadows to purify those who suffered and were distressed at what they saw going on.

"I remember well that many a time I heard our mother, enlightened by the Holy Spirit, declare that no one should pass judgment upon his neighbor unless there were question of evident sin . . . ," wrote Maconi to Pagliaresi, as he repeated that Catherine appeared before their eyes as a creature inspired by God. That abstaining from judging broke the damnable chain of rancors and dissensions that would have overcome and destroyed her brethren.

She made no distinction of persons: women or men, by the mere fact that they are rational creatures, have the duty of becoming saints: and to this she strove to attract them. "All of us have this vocation," she reminded them. All — not just some. That incitation, "Be perfect, then, as your heavenly Father is perfect" (Mt. 5:48) is extended to everyone, not just to priests or nuns or religious. Catherine, urged on by evangelical love which knows no limits, broke through every barrier. She admitted no limits either of class or of place or of state of life. When such barriers presented themselves she overcame them and was able to gather about her persons of every class and state and age and to speak the same language of truth to sovereigns and to artisans, to homemakers and to princesses. She saw not their age or their prestige or their titles; she saw only souls — and she was at their service. The first service was to guide them to Christ, forming them according to her ideal, that took on the color of fire and blood, and adapted herself to every vocation, lay or religious.

Among the nuns she encouraged the virtues of humility, virginity, prayer; among the friars, the sacerdotal virtues. Despite some unfortunate experiences and a disappointment or two, she remained particularly devoted to Blessed Raimondo da Capua, given to her, she said, by the Blessed Virgin as her director, and to Fra Tommaso della Fonte; she prayed for them, "the two columns of the Fathers," set up for her guidance and instruction, from the beginning of her "conversion" (as she called it), hoping that they would be so united as to form two bodies with a single soul. And she succeeded in becoming not only their teacher and revered mother but more especially their disciple and daughter.

The piety which she demanded of her followers was based upon her dying to herself and renouncing all worldly things, polarized on the Crucified and made strong by the willing acceptance of suffering; a Christocentric piety which, fed by her, had no suggestion of gloom or sullenness. Quite the contrary, her disciples experienced the truth of Christ's heritage: united among themselves and with Him they enjoyed perfect happiness, so that their very attitude attracted souls. By nature Catherine was sanguine, calm, and reassuring; in this regard she carried on the tradition of Italian sainthood, of Francis of Assisi and of Colombini[2] that seemed like a delectable flowering of the smiling countryside of Tuscany and Umbria, under serene blue skies, establishing a mysterious relationship between Assisi and Siena. "Peace and delight, happiness and joy and every consolation" were, in her teaching, the natural and necessary accompaniment of the "servants of God"; such she wished her followers and all the ministers of the Church to be. She loved to sing; her voice, though rather thin, was sweet, and she put her soul into it. She sang hymns and psalms, the praises of Jesus and Mary, the sort of things that allowed the popular mind to express its burdens and its hopes.

The joy which she diffused had nothing of the noisy or banal; it was a pure effusion of the love of God in the creatures she loved for Him; it was a joy, not diversion, to use the words of Pascal. Her lightheartedness even expressed itself in joking names which her followers exchanged among themselves and bore happily. Thus, Francesca was soon dubbed "stolta Cecca"[3] a nickname she cheerfully accepted as a title of honor; likewise there were "Alessia grassotta" and "Giovanna Pazza" — all expressions of that humility which their spiritual directress tried to develop in her followers. Even in the midst of an important diplomatic mission, like that at Rome in the fall of 1379, Catherine kept up an atmosphere of lighthearted joking. And by joking she signified the death of the old Adam.

In this way, without explicitly proposing to do so, but with the spontaneity of natural growth, she had gathered around her a sort of religious community, or, more properly, a family, of which she was the inspiration and the soul, the bond and the reason for its existence; then she brought them all to Christ by making them a projection of herself, a Christocentric community. The "brigade" of her followers was a part of the Church, a sort of little Church, still on pilgrimage, in which there were men and women, young and old, ecclesiastics, nuns, laymen, married and single — a true model of contemporary society, as indeed the whole Church should be, according to Catherine's ideal. And this variety, indeed universality, of composition is not the least original of Catherine's accomplishments. Within the framework of relationships she established, in the family of love, where every thought not positively sinful burned with devotion, there were always, under Catherine's direction as teacher and mother, the relationships of a family. She was the mother of all; eventually the young men and women took to calling every priest and nun and every person advanced in age "father" and "mother," while they called each other "brother" and "sister."

She did not prescribe a rule for her community: there was only the rule of divine love and, as a matter of practice, her own will. Her will was supreme, straightforward, direct, and she imposed it by the force of love, feeling the guidance of the Holy Spirit. Her followers accepted it with joy, convinced that in obeying her they were obeying God. Her life in her Spouse sealed with impressive force her statements, "I wish" or "I command," "God does not wish and I do not wish." She gave obedience in the words, "in the name of Christ crucified and my own," thus identifying herself with God before the world, whose will is her will. And she did so before great and small.

Thus the whole family rested upon her, lived in her. Each of them, one by one, encountered crises in their lives and all of them one by one were raised from earth to heaven by those transparent hands which divine love had pierced. At Siena, at Pisa, at Florence, at Avignon, at Rome — everywhere — she imparted power; she inflamed the tepid, encouraged the wavering, gave faith to the doubtful, strengthened hearts against the world. To her, however, no one in the world gave strength — only the Crucified. That which she was to her disciples — teacher, mother, friend, counselor — Jesus Christ was to her. And just as Christ gave Himself entirely for all and for her, so she gave herself entirely for all and for Him. Her followers fed upon her wisdom, warmed themselves at her love: they lived in her as in a living host offered for the love of men.

But to be perfect her disciples must know how to detach themselves from her. One evening at Montepulciano one of her latest converts, the young Pietro di Giovanni Ventura, could not tear himself away from her. At the threshold of the convent of St. Agnes she was taking leave of those about her and she felt a love for him that, though entirely pure, still had something of the human about it. "Mother," he whispered; and the others probably drew apart a little, sensing his perturbation, which everyone of them had probably experienced himself some time in the past . . . "for the love of God, I beg you to think of me tonight and ask the Lord to grant me some consolation." "I shall pray for you to the holy Virgin," Catherine replied, with a maternal smile. She looked upon him tenderly and turned him over to Mary.

If a disciple fell by the wayside or withdrew from the company she would not forget him; she followed him until he returned to her and to God; and she never stopped praying for him. Once a soul had come into contact with her, even though he was inconstant, he always came back, as if on a leash. Such was the case of Malavolti who, after repeated falls and repentances, upon the death of his wife had become a religious at Monte Oliveto, at the suggestion of Catherine. If anyone was compelled by circumstances to leave the company he could not wait to return. And if she herself were absent, they would gather in her name and, while recalling her teachings, would strive to increase in holiness and in the love of each other, according to the ideal she had inculcated. They would beg her to give them instructions so as to have occasion to obey her and in this obedience to find themselves again, for without her they were like lost sheep.

And it was Catherine's particular desire that her followers, even though away from her, would gather for mutual edification, without losing time in idle conversation and petty gossip about each other, "eating the flesh of one's neighbor" in murmurings and false judgments, but rather standing united in the name of Christ, speaking of His goodness, of the virtues of the saints, and of their own defects.

A holy virgin generally appears to good men as a copy of Mary — another Mary. Such certainly Catherine must have seemed to them, in her angelic purity, her tender motherhood, her intimacy with Christ, filled with many graces. The proof was the irresistible attraction which drew to her, and through her to Christ, such widely different souls. Whatever there was of the generous, the pure, and the beautiful in Christianity especially in Italy in the fourteenth century, seemed to gather about her, or to spring from that furnace of fire and blood. In her presence her followers, including priests and nuns, were enchanted, because they could drink at that font of wisdom which flowed from the love of God and they experienced such happiness that they tried to be with her as much as possible. Catherine, on the other hand, who loved them only for God, the only Reality, mobilized them and moved them around as sentries and knights of that army drawn up in battle array, which was her concept of the Church. They did not relish being separated from her and from one another. She, however, separated them for the love of the Crucified, dispersing them when need be for the work of the apostolate, yet keeping them bound to her in supernatural union. "We must," she declared, "do for the love of God as the Apostles did who, having received the Holy Spirit, separated from one another and from their beloved Mother, Mary. We can well imagine what a joy it would have been for them to remain together in Jerusalem; yet they sacrificed this joy to seek the glory of God and the salvation of souls. . . . This is the rule that we must follow. I realize that my presence is a consolation; nevertheless, as really obedient children, you must not seek your own consolation but rather the glory of God and the good of souls; so as not to yield to the demon who tempts you to think that you have lost my love and affection. . . ."

She loved as Christ Himself persons as bodies and souls, and therefore she was ever ready to assist them in body and soul. However, she always added, lest this love should take on an appearance merely sentimental or human: "be certain of this that I love you only because of God."

Hence, if such seemed to be the will of God, she withdrew from them whenever circumstances seemed to require. Her words, just quoted, refer to a circumstance in which the apostolate had taken her to the Val d'Orcia, in the wild country of Rocca di Tentannano, from which the Salimbeni descended like vultures and thence returned, knowing themselves invulnerable there, after their pillagings and slayings. She had gone up to that rough country to bring about peace in an internecine war. And she wrote to her companions: "You are in Siena, and Cecca and Nonna are at Montepulciano. Fra Bartolomeo and Fra Matteo will soon be with you if they are not already there. Alessia and Monna Bruna are at Monte Giovi . . . with the Contessa and Madonna Lisa. Fra Raimondo and Fra Tommaso and Monna Tomma and Lisa and I are at the Rocca, among outlaws. . . ."

And she added: "The honor of God and the salvation of souls" can be furthered . . . among those outlaws! "You must not wish for anything else. . . . Doing thus you could not possibly render more service to the eternal will of God and my own. Courage, then, my daughters, begin now to sacrifice your own will to that of Almighty God."

Thus by her own example, and holding before them the ideal of Mary, she formed her followers into handmaidens of the Lord, ready in all things to do His will. So they worked with her or under her direction communicating her spirit and stirring up love in the hearts of those whom they approached. Catherine herself could write: "They are so attached to us that they will not let us go and they literally weep at our departure."

Those young people responded, with a certain uneasiness and almost fear, to virginal love. In only one of them, however, so far as we know, did this sentiment become sinful. A religious, Fra Pietro, son of Lando, careless in his interior life, conceived a passionate love for Catherine. Despairing at not being able to overcome this guilty attraction, he planned to murder her in church. The decision would indicate that he was mentally unbalanced rather than evil. Someone — probably one of Catherine's followers — divined his intention and reproached him savagely; whereupon like another Judas, he left the church and "in a certain thicket" hanged himself. Perhaps other young followers of Catherine also experienced temptation; if so they overcame it; for with her there seemed to be no other alternative — either holiness or self-destruction.

Certainly most of her disciples followed the path of holiness. Upon her deathbed she assigned to each one of her female followers a way of perfection according to one or another of the religious rules, to take the place of her personal direction. Like the followers of St. Clare of Assisi, the disciples of Catherine in large part achieved the title of Saint. Among these known as Blessed of her followers there are Raimondo da Capua, Stefano Maconi, Guglielmo Flete, Tommaso Caffarini, Giovanni delle Celle, Giovanni Opizzenghi (a nobleman of Pisa, a Carthusian), Giovanni di Gabriele Piccolomini, Chiara Gambacorti, Bartolomeo Serafini (Prior of the Carthusian Monastery of Gorgona), and others, the crown and glory of the Saint of Siena.

NOTES:  Chapter 16

1. Literally "la brigate spendereccia," a society of Italian gentlemen toward the end of the thirteenth century who devoted themselves to lavish social parties.
2. Blessed Giovanni Colombini (1304–1367) Sienese, founder of the Jesuates.
3. It is difficult in English to do justice to the Italian idiom of these nicknames. Cecca is an archaic diminutive of Francesca; stolta means "silly," "foolish"; Alessia grassotta would be "plump Alessia"; Giovanna pazza would be "mad insane Giovanna" — Giovanna's husband's family name means literally "insane."

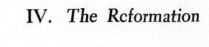

IV. The Reformation

# 17. Catherine's Mystical Exaltation

"Sleeping, eating, speaking, and in every other thing we do, we are marching toward death"; thus Catherine reminds the father of Barduccio, Piero Canigiani of Florence, one of the many Christians who, too much occupied with worldly things, live in the world as if they were always to be here.

Life is a march toward death. But the Christian makes it a march toward life. He must die to himself so as to live in God. Others, on the contrary, are dead to God because they live for themselves.

Man, in the teaching of Catherine, following the ascetic of the Prophets and the Fathers, is a wayfarer who follows the path of his existence under the constant threat of death for a period of time that is uncertain but certainly brief. How is he to overcome the terror that threatens and brings his brief existence into the orbit of the Eternal? How is he to confront the lethal forces arrayed against him?

Almost in every letter she wrote, Catherine of Siena, outlined a rule of life, the distillation of her asceticism. And it is to be noted that she considers this rule to be suitable for everybody. In writing to Piero Canigiani, for example, she says, among other things: "Conduct yourself just as would a real pilgrim, because we are all pilgrims and wayfarers in this life. . . . Neither peace nor war impedes the true pilgrim. So I wish it to be with you. Arise then, pilgrim, shake off sleep for this is not the hour for sleeping. . . . Cast off the thoughts and the cares of the world and take up the burden of the Cross, so that you will have that with which to defend yourself against the enemies you will encounter along the way. Let the blood of determination fill your heart. . . . Place God before the eye of your intellect, him Who is your end and your goal. . . ."

If God is our objective, since God is the way and the life, the end of our pilgrimage is not death. And if He is the way, this way is to be cleared of adversaries of all sorts: the march is a military maneuver, for the Church is militant. Hence Catherine — a fragile woman, frequently laid low by sickness — demands courage or, as she says, virility as opposed to servile fear. And she demands it of the Pope, of the Cardinals, of the Bishops, of the heads of government, of the common people — of everybody. Writing to a Franciscan tertiary of Genoa, she urges continuous and persistent prayer, "and then we shall be virile, because there will remain in us no feminine softness which makes for a wavering heart." A woman of virile character, a contemplative whose heart beats with the heart of Christ, she abhors "mental somnolence," inertia of will and of action.

The Christian finds himself in a constant struggle against the devil and the flesh, against riches and luxuries, stirred to the conflict by the vigor of the blood of Christ. His will is firm, he denies himself, he identifies his will with the will of God, which never vacillates. This losing one's own will in that of God is a free act accomplished in the light of reason and by no means implies fatalism; on the contrary, it implies an assiduous seeking of the divine will, a seeking to which Catherine gives the name of *perseverance* and *patience*, that is, the virtue which unswervingly resists hostile attacks, overcoming them by the force of good.

The soul of man is sought out by the devil as booty to plunder; he first seeks to undermine it through the sensitive will; this must be destroyed because the will of God controls it. Man, therefore, with the light of faith and of reason, must be continually on guard lest there penetrate into this spirit even the least thought that is not of God. Reason supervenes like an eagle to challenge the weakness of sensuality the moment it appears. Hatred of vice and love of virtue: here is the perennial war undertaken by the Christian who, like an armed knight, never ceases to oppose every impulse of the flesh, every suggestion of self-love. To this end he embraces renunciation and penance, not, however, to the point of damage to his health, for the body is an instrument designed to help the soul.

Victory in this agonizing struggle can be obtained only by the complete despoiling of one's self. This emptying of the ego is a reasoned act, to be freely decided upon and carried out; it is motivated by knowledge of self. To know one's self, what one really is, this is the first act, the foundation of Catherine's ascetic; it is the essence of medieval wisdom, expressed by Dante in *The Inferno*.

> Not to exist like brutes, but made ye
> To follow virtue and intelligence (XXVI, 119, 120).

To know and to love: these are the bases of that reform of the spirit that begins precisely with the elimination of the old Adam; no longer is self to be the center of the universe and the object of worship, God is to be this center and this object. The act was all the more necessary considering that, in the fourteenth century, there had been formed a capitalist bourgeoisie, accompanied by the rise of an urban economy based upon money, the decadence of individual and social morality, the decadence of ecclesiastical discipline and the expansion of a laic and anticlerical literature inspired and dominated by the pagan renaissance. Egocentricity and exaggerated individualism, while corroding Christian universality, with its consciousness of the brotherhood of men in the solidarity of the Mystical Body, furnished the material for the anthropocentricism of dawning humanism, to transfer worship from God to ego, dragging down man's chief interest from heaven to earth. So powerful is this egoism that from it will emerge the exploitation of men by him who becomes strongest, thus bringing about modern unrestrained capitalism, while ethical individualism will become religious individualism that will smash the unity of the Church just as nationalism will destroy the unity of Europe.

Catherine sees the dangers; she foresees the new paganism and predicts the coming schism. For this reason she hammers away at a reformation that must begin within each man's soul with knowledge of himself. She invites all — from her mother, Lapa, to her niece, Nanna, from the queen of Naples to the ladies of Milan, from the papal legate to the Abbot of Vallombrosa, from the King of France to the Pope at Avignon — to take account of their own individual nothingness to the end that they might find themselves, the real being, in God and from God. As a consequence she opposes egoism to the love that frees the soul of its own "particular" to let it expand into the infinite: that love which, for analogous reasons, had been rekindled and diffused in recent generations by a Francis of Assisi who complained that divine Love went unloved, and by a Giovanni Colombini, who reminded the nuns of Santa Bonda that "he who does not love does not live."

Thus Catherine went about firing the Christian revolution with the only combustible she was made of — love. And love, like fire, always renews itself; like blood, it is always circulating. It is the very essence of God; and hence of life itself. Love brought creatures from the bosom of the Father; it redeemed them with the Blood of the Son; it keeps them in the communion of brothers.

If love is life, hatred is death; and man has need of both; hatred of himself, love of God. Catherine repeats clearly the Augustinian motive of the two loves, and points out that the worship of the ego means the death of the soul: to love one's self is to love nonbeing.

To the real knowledge of one's self is always joined the knowledge of God: taken by itself, the former would simply discourage us; taken by itself the latter might make us proud; taken together, they establish equilibrium. In substance Catherine seeks the knowledge of self in God. To know God is to discover that He is love and that He has created us and redeemed us through love: "a mad and ineffable love"; in return He wants our love. However, God, who is infinite omnipotence, actually has no need of man's love. And He explained His motive to Catherine herself, saying to her: "I ask that you love Me with the love wherewith I have loved you. But you really cannot do so, for the reason that I have loved you without having been loved by you. You love Me as a matter of duty, not of mere willingness; that is to say, you have the obligation of loving Me. I, on the contrary, love you because I will to do so, not because I owe it to you. You cannot, therefore, repay my love; and for this reason I have given you a means to do so — your fellow man — so that you may render to him what you cannot render to Me, to will of yourself to love him, not expecting any return. And I reckon as being done to Me what you do to him."

Thus the two great commandments come into play: the second, which prescribes the love of neighbor, is similar to the first, which teaches the love of God.

We are born to love; in this lies the very substance of Christian living, in which all the virtues spring from love. We must know God because we must love; and God is love. "He who does not know himself cannot know God; and not knowing God, he cannot love; and not loving Him, he cannot arrive at perfect charity or at hatred of himself."

Love, however, also demands faith. He who loves, believes. He who loves is faithful to the loved one and serves him even unto death. But because he cannot serve God directly, for God has no need of the services of men, he serves Him through an intermediate by serving men, created by God for love.

When the mystery of love has been grasped and faith has been acquired one understands how everything that God gives or does or permits in this life, He gives or does or permits for our good. Since He is the highest good and hence can do no evil, if He sends or permits temptations, sufferings, doubts, He sends or permits them as remedies to purify us: remedies that we must therefore accept from His hands as gifts for our spiritual health. Then when our life has been conformed to the divine will we shall be established in peace. Man is like a candle to be lighted — to be lighted in God. The combustible material is love. As the heavenly Father will say to Catherine: "Your material is love because I have created you for love; hence without love you cannot live." Without love one must die: a lamp without oil goes out.

This light is lighted day by day above all at the flame of the Eucharist, sacrament of love. "The soul," Jesus will say on another occasion to Catherine, "receiving this Sacrament lives in me and I in it: like a fish lives in the sea and the sea in the fish, thus I live in the soul and the soul in Me — a tranquil sea." They err who abstain from the Bread of Angels under the pretext of being unworthy, as if anyone could be worthy! On the contrary, it is the Sacrament itself which makes us worthy, if we approach it with the right intention.

To love is to insert one's self in the nature of God, who is the way, the truth, and the life, who is goodness and peace. To accumulate virtues and merits is not enough, as it is not enough to gather combustible materials: to have warmth one must light them; and what lights them is love.

All the strivings of theologians and diplomats and preachers and missionaries are to no avail if they do not lead to love. By loving, one gives the life of God to the loved one. As St. John of the Cross will say: "Where you do not find love, implant love and you will find love." And Christ said to Catherine: "He who knows himself to be loved cannot do otherwise than love; in loving he will put on the spirit of Christ crucified, and in the tempestuous sea of many troubles he will find himself at peace." Love God and do the will of God; made one with God who, since He is love is also strength, he will joyfully face up to adversities. Thus love will be "that virtue that never loses sight of the will of God: it is strong, it is never conquered, but always conquers. . . ."

Hence it is that Christ could declare: I have overcome the world. And at the conclusion of his struggle the Christian should be able to say the same. He must overcome adversity, not submit to it but make use of it to fashion the material of love; this is precisely why he is in the world. Tribulations ("the treasure of tribulation") constitute the lesson, the "sweet discipline" by which God fashions us. Borne with adherence to God's will, they will always be productive of good. And adherence to the divine will implies also that man must not try to determine either the time or the place for his trials but will rest content with God's choice of these circumstances. Furthermore, tribulations are part of those "transitory things that pass as the wind and matter little, either what they are to us or we are to them." A will which denies itself and is transformed in God is disposed to bear sufferings and trials in whatever way God gives them: He gives them "because of His great love, for He cannot wish anything else but our sanctification." Under this aspect tribulations are necessary; without them we should certainly fall.

As for herself, Catherine, in the footsteps of Christ offers to take upon her own shoulders also the tribulations of her brethren, so that they may be freed from any fault. She considers as of the same value honor and scorn, joys and sorrows, and she deals with them alike in the satisfaction of doing the will of the Father. Christ's proof of His love for us was the shedding of His blood; our proof of our love for others is to give our blood for our brethren loved by Christ.

This rallying about the cross to be united to God and to become one with Him, thus becoming strong in the life of God by mystical contemplation and ascetical renunciation, this radical detachment from the world and complete preoccupation with the Supreme Good, all this is Catherine's revolutionary reaction against the religious decadence of her times, when ecclesiastics were sunk in worldliness, scholars stooped to twaddle, statesmen inclined to laicism and men of letters embraced paganism: an entire social order withdrawn from the Redemption and dedicated to the flesh pots of Egypt, under the influence of a humanism become slave to man's lower instincts within and to political absolutism without.

It was a severe ascetic, to be sure: without compromise, because it demanded a life of the cross, a dying to one's self. It was a burning desire for martyrdom, for the shedding of blood; it was a losing of self for the rebirth of the Church. Catherine demanded of each disciple, down to the last, a life enclosed in the heart, "to live as if dead," in poverty, in humility, in patience, and in prayer: "Rid yourselves of every indulgence toward yourselves and of every servile fear," because, as she never tired of repeating, "the Church has no need of weaklings but of persons who are cruel to themselves, devoted to her."

As she demanded of herself, so she demanded of each disciple: "Offer your life; do not give yourself a moment of repose." "God, from the beginning of the world to its end, has willed and wills that no great accomplishment may ever be reached without great trials."

Thus she expresses that ardor of greatness, so essential to the real Christian: the greatness of Jesus Christ as He mounted the cross, the ladder to divine heights.

The honor of God, the sacrifice of self: this is Catherine's program — a red-hot blade wielded by a feeble body.

## 18. *The Spiritual Directress*

In almost every one of her letters to her disciples their spiritual mother hammered away at this teaching of the cross. To Nicolo Soderini, after a forage of the Ciompi in which his properties had been sacked and burned, Catherine wrote out a lesson of patience — of strength — which is an orderly summary of this teaching.

"Sin is the only thing of which we should grow weary; of nothing else, because by sin we lose the only thing that is really ours. What do we lose? Grace, which is the blood of Christ, which is our life, which cannot be taken from us either by the devil or by any earthly creature unless we so will. But there are other things — riches, honors, state of life, pleasures, bodily health and life and any other thing — because they are not really ours but are given to us to use according to the will of the good God, these can be taken away. But we must not thereby be troubled, must not grow impatient, but must give them up without regret; we must be prepared to relinquish whatever is not really ours. Surely we must see that no man can hold these things in the way he might wish; so it is better to give them up; indeed, either they are taken away from us or we are taken away from them by death. Things being as they are, that man is stupid and insane who allows in himself a miserable and disordered affection for them.

"It befits a strong man to cleanse his heart of attachment to any transitory thing, and for the love of Christ to embrace the holy cross, where we shall find ineffable love refreshed by the blood of Christ, where we shall find the patience of the humble and immaculate Lamb. We shall see that with the same tender love with which he has given His life for us, He also gives us and permits every trial and tribulation as well as consolation that comes to us." Thus the problem of suffering is solved; the mystery of life is clarified; fear is vanquished by love.

This brief life must be spent quickly but well. Laziness is a grave sin; hence we see Catherine exhorting persons dear to her, even though they be ill, even though they be completely dedicated to God, not to be lazy; indeed we see her sometimes commanding them to rise from their sickbeds, to leave their retirement and to go labor in the Lord's vineyard. The contemplative burns with the fever of action — not because she is spurred by the presentiment of death but rather because she realizes so well the waste that most persons make of this one and ephemeral value which is our earthly existence, lived thoughtlessly by all too many, as if they were never to die or as if life here below were the sum total of existence.

An imaginative and powerful expression of hers tells how she understands the Christian use of our existence: "If we could really see the Crucified," she wrote to Stefano Maconi, "our heart would burn with the fire of love, and we would be starved for time."

Particularly acute is her realization of the value of such time as is exclusively ours to dispose of: that which we call the present moment, what Fenelon called "a little eternity," what Sister Elizabeth of the Trinity called "the eternal present." The only part of time that is securely at our disposal is this present moment in which we speak or think or work or rest. "The moment that is past you have no more; you are not sure of any future moment; you have only the present moment, nothing more," she writes to Maconi. "Only the present moment exists, and nothing else," she writes to the merchant, Marco Bindi, who perhaps thought that time is like money. Catherine shows that in a certain sense time is eternity: certainly it is the greatest value affecting our eternal destiny. To live, then, the present moment to the full is to live as God lives. As Dante says:

> Thus do contingent things before the event
> Exist for thee, still gazing where take head
> All times together with the present blent.
> (*Paradiso*, XVII, 16)

At this actual moment — therefore at once — Catherine requires of each one his sanctification; it is for this that the Creator has given him existence. "It is simple truth that His will is our sanctification; for this end did God create us" — she writes to the noble Trinci family of Foligno. Each one can become holy in his own state of life: the mother of a family, by being a good mother; the virgin by living the beauty of virginity; married persons by practicing the holiness of marriage. To the more generous of the last-mentioned she suggested that they pass "from the imperfect state of marriage to the state of angelic continence, which is perfect." To Ristoro Canigiani and his wife she writes: "rise above mere human living and take up a life that is angelic; to this you are called by God. Correspond generously to His grace and you will be an angelic couple upon earth."

Dedicated so completely to God, since God is everything and we owe everything to Him, she demands of each follower the same complete dedication: "No one who puts his hand to the plow and then looks back is fit for the kingdom of God" (Lk. 9:62). "Leave the dead to bury their own dead" (Mt. 8:22). Parents who oppose the vocations of their children forget that a state of life is to be chosen not in their way but in God's way; they do even worse when they resort to religious sophisms, presuming to correct the designs of the Holy Spirit.

As to statesmen, she does not ask that they abandon politics but only that they govern with firmness and justice, as dependent upon God and at the service of their fellow men. To the Knights of Rhodes[1] she recommended campaigning as virile knights, using love as their principal weapon — for love, she declared, is the most powerful weapon in existence; they should consider as their worst enemies vice, the world, sensuality; only then should they resort to material arms. Advocates she advised not to resort too easily to courts of law and not to resort to legal technicalities and always, like St. Yves[2] to succor the rights of the poor. She recommended to the rich that they sell their superfluous wealth and give the proceeds to the needy, to divest themselves of lavish vesture, clothing themselves and their households according to necessity, "honestly," as she put it.

In the fields of economics and political science Catherine imparted norms drawn from the Gospels and the purest traditions of the Fathers of the Church, and enlivened by her own experience. Kingdoms, states, civil power, and riches, all these, just as one's children and friends and every other worldly thing are the property of God and are entrusted to men for their use, as administrators, as a sort of loan, not a gift. Their end is the honor of God, the development of the Church, the salvation of souls. Hence, men must use them as dispensers or representatives of Christ crucified. Riches are given — or rather lent — for the ultimate good of the poor. Addressing the rich and powerful, Catherine castigates those egotists who dissipate wealth in riotous living and consign to hunger the poor, in whom they ought to see God. Her predilection for the poor is apparent and when she turns her attention to the rich it is that she may make them poor in spirit, induce them to renounce the world — even though they be reigning monarchs, so that they may live as servants of the Crucified, faithful dispensers of the good conferred by the Father of all.

Thus, since all worldly goods come from God, let them return to God and, precisely, let them return to God through our neighbor; Catherine held that the rich should perform this social service. It is of heroic counsel to give one's goods to the poor; however, one may "with due care" conserve them "in good conscience," for man is not bound to alienate his property beyond a certain limit, although it is true that if he does so he attains a greater perfection. The essential thing is to place one's self in the sight of God in performing any act. In short, the Christian, if he have worldly goods and position, may retain them, provided he does not hold on to them "with disordered love." "And thus, in whatever state he be — gentleman or noble, high in political position or worldly wealth, living in perfect chastity or in marriage, having children or without them, in every state he can be pleasing to God, just so he love. . . ."

Love remains: it can value even the riches which the Christian ethic normally rejects, for we are exhorted to use the goods of this world to make friends in heaven. Without love, however, everything else is meaningless.

Radical and demanding though she be regarding the cultivation of virtue, Catherine is never extreme or fanatic. Her flame is regulated by the light of reason and fed by love, a love that is itself "orderly," and, therefore, not such as to permit the soul to harm itself in order to do good to another or even to the whole world together, for one may never commit the slightest sin to promote a great virtue. This was her specific message to the political heads of the city of Bologna.

In substance she demanded the same conduct — renunciation of the world, freedom from servile fear, the service of God — from the powerful and from artisans; from the noble woman, Laudomia degli Strozzi of Florence; and from the hermit, Niccolo Povero of the Romagna; from Neri di Landoccio; and from the Archbishop of Florence. High placed persons, also, must become poor — at least in spirit — and must embrace the cross. She demanded substantially the same thing of a prostitute, calling her "my very dear daughter," and confiding her to the Blessed Virgin.

As may be seen, it is a violent breaking away from unworthy ties, a decisive rupture of old habits that Catherine demands of all alike, to desert the deceitful world for the faithful God. Life is short, and one may not hesitate in choosing between God and the world, between life eternal and death eternal. Her model is the Crucified, who by His teachings and His example, spurs us on "to love the honor of God and the salvation of souls; and by sufferings, by doing violence to our own sensuality, to acquire virtue." She inculcates heroism in the battle against the world and the flesh and self-love, and the free acceptance of sufferings as a true refreshment of the soul. She demands a love that delights in and is tempered by pain, an abandonment in the blood which flows from the thorn-crowned head of Christ crucified.

Catherine's apostolate, based upon a few fundamental principles, does not always appear externally in the same guise; it may always be reduced to the color of blood and of fire, but beyond this it adapts itself to the varying circumstances of the souls to whom she directs her attention. It conforms itself completely to the needs of each person, tends to supernaturalize vocation and the state of life of each soul. This all-embracing quality, which tends to make Catherine's apostolate universal, is effective wherever it operates, for the renovation of the Church — in homes, in places of business, in monasteries, in political life, in Bishops' palaces, on the thrones of kings, in libraries, in the pulpit, in the studios of artists.

Catherine, one of the most complete mystics that have adorned the Church, all the while she enjoyed heavenly contemplation, still penetrated this worldly ambient to the point of bringing to light its most hidden miseries; she engaged in the humblest of services, from giving medical assistance to gathering funds for the Crusade, from seeking historical documents from the Vatican library to collecting bread and alms for the needy. And when her brothers who had migrated to Florence, importuned their mother, Lapa, for financial assistance, Catherine reminded them, through her eldest brother, of the obligations of children toward their parents; they had forgotten, she said, the debt of existence and sustenance they owed her, but were actually and shamelessly making renewed demands upon her. Children, she reminded them, have only obligations to the parents, not rights to enforce against them.

Catherine speaks to her brothers with a sort of loving sadness, reminds them of their obligations to God and to their mother, insists upon their duty of loving God and accepting the trials He sends them. She attempts to revive their hopes, for "when human aid is lacking the aid of God is near."

Daughter and mother, bold and intrepid, of the Church and of the Pope, she makes her own the interests of God; her heart is that of the Church itself; she makes clear to all the needs of "the universal body of the Christian religion" and of "The Mystical Body of Holy Church." In this vision she makes her own the needs of all men redeemed by Christ.

We may note one outstanding fact in Catherine's apostolate of direction and formation: that if, by her love, Catherine is principally in the tradition of St. Francis of Assisi, by her passion for truth she is rather in the steps of St. Dominic Guzman. In her spirit, love and truth are one: she loves to speak the truth to all. One who lives up to the truth faces the light, so that everybody can see that his life is lived in union with God (Jn. 3:21). Illumined by the Holy Spirit, she grows in the holiness of truth — the ultimate expression of love. "O God, give me the grace to be ever the lover and herald of truth, and for this truth I shall gladly give my life." Pinpointing her concept, she discovers that hers is a "cordial love founded in truth," in which heart and reason merge; as in the Gospel of St. John, where Jesus is constantly presented as truth and love.

Her character is, through love, an attractive femininity and, through her will, a powerful virility. That "I will" of hers still retains, down through the centuries, something of the mysterious power with which it was first pronounced. Since her will was identified with the will of God, she commanded with authority and, one might almost say, with the infallibility of God Himself, and no discussion is tolerated. After all, one does not argue about the truth.

With this will of hers Catherine has a grasp of values such as few have had, without however becoming congealed in an inhuman voluntarism, rather integrating will with love, sentiment with reason. "What is it that fortifies our soul and weakens our enemies? It is our will, vested by love with the sweet will of God; a will that is so potent that neither the demon nor any creature can weaken it unless it wishes. And why is it so strong? Because it is voluntarily united to God, Who is absolute and eternal strength." Like God, then, who is unchangeable, one can become firm and unwavering. Love aids, nourishes, and fashions the will. In fact, as she explains to her disciple, Ristoro Canigiani — not only is love not a mere pose, a changeable attitude, but it is humble, not proud; it is faithful and prudent but it is also just and strong. So she insists upon strength, for it is this which will render the spirit invincible by investing it with grace. "Whence we see that if our neighbor injures us and we bear the injury with patience, the poisoned thrust boomerangs upon the offender. If the world assails us with its pleasures, its delights and its promises and we reject them, the world is weakened even as it hates us. And if the demon grieves us with his many and varied temptations we overcome him with the force of our will, remaining firm, constant and persevering until death, refusing assent to his wiles. While we stand fast in this way no sin can come to us, for only the will can commit sin. . . ."

As she remarked to a Pope who was strong and, for that matter, violent, Urban VI: "God is our strong fortress; who stands in love stands in God and God in him, for God is love." In Him love gains the character of strength; it is life and health and truth. He who loves stands in God and will not fall. Catherine can say with Jesus Christ: I have overcome the world (Jn. 16:33).

NOTES: *Chapter 18*

1. Members of the Military Order of St. John.
2. St. Yves, Bishop of Chartres (1040–1116), patron saint of lawyers; compiled a collection of Canon Law.

# 19. The Reformer

One of the highest of Catherine's objectives is the reform of the Church. She is quite aware of the wounds which the body of the Mystical Christ has suffered and she makes no attempt to hide them. She knows the sins and vices through which have come about "such ruin and harm and irreverence of the Church and her ministers," she will have Fra Raimondo speak about them to the Pope. She is prepared to do battle against any and every moral evil, convinced that only by a purifying of minds and morals can the fortunes of the Church — including those merely temporal — be rebuilt.

And since all are members of the Mystical Body, the reform must be initiated by each individual. Hence Catherine attempts to sanctify herself and her followers. Wherefore, every hour of the day is to be spent in freeing the Mystical Body of the incrustations of sin whence it suffers; especial attention is given to religious, to "the anointed of the Lord, to ecclesiastical officials, who must bear the primary responsibility for the decadence"; wherever she goes, with words of hope, when she discovers decay she points it out and tries to remove it.

With this in view she is severe with herself and her followers, she demands that parents be holy, that children be docile, that artisans be honest, that rulers be upright, that Franciscans be true Franciscans, that Dominicans live according to the ideal of St. Dominic, that all religious become fragrant flowers in the garden of Holy Church. Artificers and accomplices in the ruin of the Church are those religious men and women who no longer live according to their rule, who have lost their love for their cells. He is the only true religious who offers the dowry of his free will to his Spouse at the moment of his religious profession, who considers the glory and the richness of poverty, in which and for which he has no occasion to maintain relations with those who do not serve God but rather avoids the common temptations, as he serves his brethren, without any hope of recompense, because he loves them for God's sake and not for himself or for themselves. "Vest yourselves with sufferings and opprobrium for Him," she advises the nuns of San Pietro in Monticelli; "unite and love one another." The communion of souls is the flood tide of love, a circulation of the divine blood; it heals and vivifies.

Disciplined in this strict ascetic, souls conform themselves to the Crucified, accepting, with Him, insults, persecution, sufferings, crushing, their self-love and clearing their mind of fantasies to open it to virtues. The true nuns, she tells Tora, the future Chiara Gambacorti, are servants and spouses of Jesus crucified; they withdraw from the world, without ever returning to it even in thought, considering even such return a sort of adultery, a love apart from God, even if there be a question of love for father, mother, sister or brother or relatives or riches or worldly state. The true spouse loves no one and nothing but Christ; she loves virtue; she hates all that He hates. Her virtues are tested by her love of her neighbor. She despises vice. She does not waste time, but is always busied in prayer, in reading or in manual labor, so as not to fall into idleness.

Spiritual directress, former of consciences, Catherine knows the pitfalls of the religious life; she knows of its crises of tepidity, its repugnance to obedience and to silence, its dangers of confusion and desperation. For this reason she recalls and heals the spirits of her followers by establishing them in love. She inflames them with fire and blood; she uproots them from self-love to hurl them into hatred of self and into love of God; she figuratively nails them to the cross. She traces out the beginnings of pride and binds them to a radical humility which delights in being subject not only to superiors but also to inferiors, making them the servants of all. Catherine shows them how to make fruitful use of temptations and trials of every sort: by abandoning themselves, with a will dead to the world, into the hands of God and of one's superiors. She knows the benefits of a humility that has been invigorated by sins and errors into which one has fallen but risen again. She knows the periods of tedium at prayer in the cell, of sensual and worldly appetites, and even the loss of time that one endures at recreation with other religious or in the visiting room with callers, in conversation with devoted followers, in spiritual friendships. Out of that thicket of subtle habits and thoughts and temptations she will have flowers not brambles.

She realizes the power of the bond that unites religious in their common life and she wants them to feel united in it, so as even to form one unity: and "this is the sign that God left to his disciples," she writes to the spiritual sons of Giovanni delle Celle[1] warning them against certain tendencies toward individualism.

Naturally, as a Dominican religious, she had particularly at heart the rejuvenation of the Dominicans. The state of the Order did not escape her. She asked the Pope that if the general of the Order, Fra Elia da Tolosa, was to be removed that His Holiness would appoint to the post "a good and virtuous man," the real need would be filled. Later on it will be the task of her disciple, Blessed Raimondo, to carry out the reform when, in 1380, after her death, he will be named Master General of the Order of Preachers.

For the benefit of her niece, Eugenia, a Dominican nun in the convent of Sant' Agnese at Montepulciano, Catherine, in a letter which was a sort of small treatise, minutely delineates the figure of the spouse of Christ; stripped of herself, lost in the will of God, obedient to all, totally dedicated to Jesus Christ, a jealous Spouse. She loves only God; how foolish, then, would her love be should she abandon the Creator for creatures. Hence, she should not give her heart to anything or anyone except the Crucified. To safe-guard her purity, let her avoid particular contacts either with reli-gious (even confessors) or with seculars (even though through the grating of the cloister). Woe to Eugenia (whom, though about Catherine's age, the aunt treated as a daughter, and disciple) if word of any such thing would come to Catherine's ears; although Montepulciano is quite far away her aunt would inflict such punishment upon her as to cause her never again to forget herself. (And let Eugenia remember that her aunt could read souls even across mountain ranges.) As to prayer, recalling ideas already grasped by her niece and experiences she had had, Catherine insists that it be continuous (every thought and action throughout the day must be directed to God and done in His honor); that it be vocal (the Divine Office and other prescribed prayers); and that it be mental (in which the mind rises above itself and is united to God).

With a criterion equally austere, radical, and liberating she directs the married and the single, whom she also would have saints, as monks without a monastery, adorned with the same virtues, the first of which must be love. She inculcates everyday duties: faith with good works, among which is the restitution of super-fluous wealth to the divine Goodness, that is, to the poor; purity of mind in daily affairs; chastity in married life. She knows that parents are always preoccupied about the temporal welfare of their children and their future well-being; she recommends confidence in divine Providence, which never fails. Thus she purifies their minds, reassures them, by unveiling before their eyes the power that can conquer the world.

Though all the evangelical virtues are exalted in her teaching, the character of the times impelled her to put special emphasis upon poverty. She began by practicing it herself. In the midst of a family relatively well off, she lived in poverty, accepting from her parents only those things which they would allow her to give to the poor. So much did she love this virtue, the benefits of which were all the more apparent to her as she beheld the harm that riches wrought in the bosom of the Church, that she prayed that those near and dear to her would be reduced to poverty. When they will have become poor, she reasoned, they will be more humble, they will seek spiritual riches, and be more dependent upon God. And the Lord heard her, for through the political and economic crises which Siena experienced, with the failing fortunes of the artisan class, the Benincasa family were reduced to such straits that some of them emigrated to Florence. Catherine encouraged them and comforted them in their trials. In a letter to the Bishop of Florence, Angelo Ricasoli, surrounded by numerous prelates immersed in politics and worldly affairs, Catherine recalls the obligations of charity and of courage in the ministry, the duty of conferring spiritual and temporal favors for the good of the brethren "not selling them for money or in simony," not building up their stables, not engaging in financial speculations, not squandering in riotous living the patrimony of the Church, which belongs to the poor, but rather honoring God and serving their brethren. This is the job of pastors! "Alas, alas, alas, how my soul is desolated! Today they do not conduct themselves so. But because they love venality, they love themselves for themselves and God for themselves and their neighbor, for themselves." They try to sell the Holy Spirit, they rob the honor of God, and they go unpunished. "Considerations of your salvation impel me thus to address you. . . . Remember that you must die, and you know not when."

Fearless language that she uses to cardinals and to the Pope himself; so that she felt it necessary to remark: "I shall not say more, Holy Father, except that you must pardon me, a miserable creature." However, she had spoken out.

In 1377, writing either from Siena or from Belcaro, she insists upon the urgency of reforming the highest government of the Church, removing evil pastors and naming holy ones in their place. About the same time she writes to Fra Raimondo, at Rome, that our Lord wishes first of all the reform of the Church, whose face is now all covered with the uncleanness and self-love of her errant children, swollen with pride and avarice, so that she may regain her beauty, not by the force of arms, cruelty and war, but through peace, prayer, and tears.

Her strictures become more vehement when there is question of sins of immorality. The degradation of the soul through the medium of the body seems to her the most ungrateful affront to God who has made us, body and soul, in sublime dignity. To a nobleman who had sinned against nature, while addressing with sorrowful appeals burning with virgin love and outlining with vivid strokes the danger of his dying in his sad state, she presents the figure of the flagellated Christ, against whom he, a dear but degenerate brother, has reduced his own body from a temple to a stall. "O robber, O insensible debtor," she exclaims, "God will not bear such abomination and such iniquity. . . . Are you, then, a beast, a brutish animal?" When tempted to carnal sin, let him consider the flesh of the Crucified, who by uniting divine nature with human nature raised our flesh above the choirs of angels. She concludes by remarking that if she has used words that are too strong and said things that he would have preferred not to hear, the love which she bears him must be her excuse.

Later on in her *Dialogue* she will again hurl fiery darts against perverts of this sort.

NOTE:   *Chapter 19*

1. Florentine ascetical writer, died 1396; Abbot of Vallombroso.

## 20. *Fire and Flames*

To throw a firebrand upon the earth — that is my mission! And oh, how I wish it were already in a blaze! (Lk. 12:49.) Thus Jesus spoke of Himself. And Catherine, filled with His spirit, could repeat it of herself. She declared: "My nature is a flame." She became a partaker of the very nature of God; for her God presents Himself as "fire above every fire," which, burning, does not consume. Perhaps one may best explain the ecstasies, the heroism, the apostolate, the letters, the prayers of this young nun in the light of this flame: a glowing brazier in the cold night of the world.

She was, in this regard, an incendiary, and she set fire to Italy and, indeed, to Christendom, so that she might destroy its miseries and restore its soul. "I am the fire and you are the sparks." . . . "If you really are what you are supposed to be you will set fire to all Italy," she declared to her followers and contemporaries.

She was devoured, almost to the point of death, by "hunger for the honor of God and the salvation of souls," a veritable "fire of love," and burning with it she spent herself beyond her physical powers. She was consumed in the blood of the Lamb in "a burning desire" and even her language was red-hot. She knew that life should be exploited minute by minute, without wasting a second; that death will come and it may find us in some defect: "Do not await the time for time will not wait for you," she cries; and she urges: "Rise up, then manfully!" With her there is continuous struggle, a restless thirst for souls, a tireless battle to bring the kingdom of heaven and to drive out satan — "I have come only to gain souls, to snatch them from the hands of the demon" — settling life against death, peace against war, love against hate: hate which is anti-love, death; hate which begets sin, which is nonbeing, the plunging of the soul back into the nothingness out of which it was created. A person who hates expels grace, kills his soul, reducing it to "a sack full of filth, the food of death, the food of worms."

Tedium and lukewarmness, as morbidness and a spirit of criticism, were for Catherine the chill of death. Hence her efforts to arouse faith and courage, to infuse the flame of ardor, in a supposedly Christian society prone to freeze in inertia, inclined to desperation or skepticism, to surrender in distrust. She disdained to seek repose; she made the anxieties of all her own; she never took refuge in flight, never bowed to gloom; she lived completely in faith, hope, and love. She burned with desire to shed her blood for the spouse of Christ, the Church; since she did not succeed in giving the testimony of her blood for God, she consumed herself in the testimony of love for her neighbor, for the love of God.

She is a voice crying on a battlefield upon which she launched her attack upon the enemies of Christian spirituality and of the Church. She does not turn back, she does not shun reprisals and she encourages her followers to do likewise, for such is the will of God. She has not a sword in her hands; she has only her voice for a weapon; and the passion that feeds her ardor and her belligerence is love.

Noteworthy is her centering of spirituality upon the cult of the Blood of Christ. Like a liquid flame this Blood has tinged with living purple the warp and woof of human history. One drop of this Blood, as Aquinas had sung, can save the universe.

It is because, as she recalls to Pope Gregory, the Blood was sprinkled in the fire of love; there is no blood without fire, and no fire without blood. In the sprinkling of blood we perceive the burning fire of love. "Why is fire found in blood? Because the blood was sprinkled in the more ardent fire of love."

This concept imparts that consuming ardor to Catherine's spirituality, enkindled and characterized precisely by the Blood of Christ. For the blood is the life of the body; it brings warmth, it heals, it nourishes; sprinkled with love, it represents the greatest gift, the supreme offering.

Catherine never ceases to enumerate its benefits: every letter begins and closes with the subject; her whole soul is permeated with it. Man can never be satisfied except by that Blood, because it is "permeated and shot through with divinity." From the Blood of Christ comes the grace which animates us, the warmth which gives us life, the light that enlightens us. From that Blood comes knowledge of self and hence the end of self-love, because the soul that knows itself to be loved in that Blood transfers its love from its ego to God. We imbibe the Blood of Christ as we are nourished by His Body; in no other way may our soul's hunger and thirst be satisfied.

Humanity is the receptacle into which flows the Blood that drips from the cross, just as it is the ground into which the cross is fixed. For love of us that cross was set up, Jesus was affixed to it, His Blood flowed, and still flows from it.

Catherine's prose is starred with hymns to the Blood of Christ. As she writes to the Carthusian, Pietro di Milano, "In His Blood we find the source of mercy; in His Blood, tenderness; in His Blood is the forgiveness of our sins; in His Blood, the hardness of our heart is softened; in His Blood, bitter things become sweet and heavy burdens are made light. . . . the soul that is plunged into and inebriated with that Blood takes on real and true virtues for the glory of God and realizes the truth again demonstrated by means of that Blood."

And therefore — she pursues that thought, writing to Fra Raimondo — "plunge yourself into the Blood of Christ; take it upon yourself; be remorseful in that Blood; rejoice in that Blood; grow and become strong in that Blood; get rid of your weakness and blindness in the Blood of the spotless Lamb; and in the light you will advance securely, like an armed knight, to seek the honor of God, the good of Holy Church, and the salvation of souls."

She sees the Church as the custodian, as the depository, of the Blood of Christ; she sees the Pope as the vicar of that sacrificial Lamb whose priests are responsible for ministering its Blood. Humanity will be redeemed just to the extent that it consumes and is plunged into that stream of salvation.

And even if the Pope, for whom she contends and consumes herself, were to drive her away, Catherine would take refuge in the wounds of Christ crucified whose Vicar the Pope is. And certainly Christ will receive her, as he does every sinner, and, received by Christ, how can she be rejected by His Vicar? And under His protection she will continue to fight for the sweet spouse of Christ. "In the Church," she exclaimed to the Pope "I must end my life in tears, and in sighs and sufferings, and give my blood and the marrow of my bones for her. If the whole world were to reject me I should not care; I should still find refuge there, in tears but with determination, in her bosom."

## 21. Peace and War

Catherine had discovered the key to peace in the will of God. This, for the Middle Ages was a truth luminously clear, as when Dante had written in *Paradiso:* "His will is the consummation of our peace." To her impatient mother, Lapa, the extremely patient daughter had pointed out that "the soul must be conformed to and invested with the sweet will of God; wherefore it rejoices in everything and is content with whatever happens. Hence the creature, invested with this sweet will, has lasting peace!" He is no longer disturbed; he has overcome fear, the mental illness of the age to which we rightly apply the disdainful epithet, *servile*, the fear that marks a slave.

From interior peace, eager to restore the kingdom of God upon earth, she rises to external peace — family peace, social peace, international peace. Catherine, like Francesco, like Colombini, like Christ Himself, the Mediator between the Father and men to put an end to the enmity between them, making Himself "our peace," influences individuals and families, rulers and soldiers, the king and the pope, inducing them to be reconciled, vying with one another in a contest of love.

Completely recollected, with the eye of an eagle, illumined by love, she contemplated the panorama of her contemporary world and grasped the nature of the sickness with which it was tortured: desertion of the law of God, and, therefore, war. War is the destruction of material goods and the fratricide of Christians; hence it is anti-Christian, the practical failure of the religion of love. From war come all the world's evils. Hence to the Pope, whom she sees as the vortex of a peaceful social order and the foundation of worldly peace, since in him all men can rediscover themselves as brothers, she can say: "My soul, narrowed between self and God, yearning for the salvation of men, the reform of Holy Church and the good of the whole world, can see no other remedy pleasing to God than peace. Peace, peace, therefore, for the love of Christ crucified!"

This is the will of God. And Catherine is the voice proclaiming that will, expressing it with the authority of Him who manifests it to her. "Is there any more attractive thing than peace?" she asks of Nicolo Soderini, patron of the arts, and therefore one of the authorities in that Florence which was being infected with the psychosis of war. "Is there anything more attractive than peace? Certainly not. This was the sweet legacy, the great lesson, that Jesus Christ left to His disciples. He told them: 'You will not be known as My disciples by the miracles you work, nor by divining in the future, nor by showing forth holiness in your lives, but by having charity and peace and love together.' "

She seeks to fix this truth in the minds of all those in authority with whom she comes into contact. And since it is God's truth and she feels herself "constrained by this first sweet truth," she insists upon being heard. A universal peacemaker, she fights for peace against its enemies, who are such because they are the friends of wealth and of luxury, devotees of their own ego. In the militant Church of the fourteenth century there is not a single other spirit that more vigorously makes war upon war; an archangel of light who assails the powers of darkness to give back to Christendom "the peace longed for for so many years."

Where the love of God is lacking, war is inevitable. Hence her apostolate to the heads of government culminates always in an apostolate of love. The cardinals of the papal court at Avignon, since their aim is pomp and magnificence, are the counselors of the devil, enkindling the passions of war; and logically, for corruption and war, sin and war, stand in the relation of cause and effect. Seculars, religious, clerics are avid followers of the world's uncleanness and hence of conflicts. If all the rest of corrupt humanity is gathered in the "exile of death" and in fratricidal wars fights against God, the Pope must not be caught in this universal madness, but must rise above it and bring about peace. She knows, and she says clearly, that to have peace it is necessary to clean up the highest ecclesiastical levels, driving out the "stench of unworthy ministers" and re-establishing the primacy of the spiritual. There is a necessary logical connection between reform and peace.

How can we be Christians and still make war? To be a Christian means to include our enemies in our love, to pardon indefinitely.

The Pope, who, as the sweet Christ upon earth, should be, like Christ, the peacemaker par excellence, even as Italy is desolated by mercenary troops, himself takes part in the depredations of war. Such participation seems to Catherine a monstrous thing; she begs him to assume his true office in the world. How can the father of the faithful run after titles, temporal wealth, the vanities of the world, the effect of which is the destruction of souls, the blasphemy of God — all in armed conflicts? To the objection that "the treasury of the Church" must be recovered, the virgin of Siena replies that "the treasury of the Church is the blood of Christ, shed to redeem souls," that the safeguarding of spiritual values is more necessary than safeguarding the material, observing also that even in the temporal order more fruitful results are obtained by love than by arms, and the Pope is losing both the temporal and the spiritual.

To a pagan, Catherine's reasoning might seem ingenuous; yet it impressed a man of arms such as Giovanni Hawkwood; in fact, it sounded to him much more realistic than any sort of specious political realism.

"Peace, peace, peace, for the love of God!" she repeats again and again to the Pope; and seeing how the pontiff allowed himself to be embroiled in the political machinations of powerful worldlings, she felt she was dying and wanted to die. The blood of Christians that

heads of government and of arms to give their lives fighting in the Crusade, for the name of Jesus, to find in the shedding of their blood the washing away of their sins.

To the heads of state who, trusting in the pagan tactic of *divide and conquer*, by their conduct formed the picture of Machiavelli's *Prince*,[1] Catherine, without euphemisms or beating about the bush, recalled the holy fear of God and the obligation to love: to love in order to live. And she exhorts them to the spiritual business of knowing themselves, because, knowing themselves, they will not fall into pride "either of greatness or of power." Even if he were ruler of the world the Christian must consider himself to be nothing. His power is not really his, for it may at any instant be snatched from him by death. It is rather a temporary administration entrusted to him by the one Lord. Only one city is securely confided to our power: the city of the soul, in which God reposes, rendering it impregnable unless it falls into mortal sin. In this case the ruler of the city becomes a slave, loses all his dignity. Of what use is it, therefore, to capture cities and castles if one, as a slave of evil, loses his soul?

On this theme Catherine follows the thought of St. Thomas Aquinas.[2] She holds that the administration of a city, a kingdom, or a family cannot be withdrawn from the law of the Gospel. He who governs according to this law looks after "the universal common good," and not his own particular good. So on this point Catherine's Catholic thought contrasts sharply with what will be the pagan thought of Guicciardini,[3] the defender of "special interests." Political theory in those times, as Catherine observed, deformed justice because it looked to the interests of him who governed, not to the interests of him who was governed.

It evolved not from the "light of reason" but from the passion of hatred, factiously, as if there were not an eternal Judge who will apply the *lex talionis*, the law of retaliation. As a conscientious citizen Catherine outlines for civil rulers the ideal type of "just ruler," intent upon "the universal and common good of the whole realm." And her fellow citizens understood well the direction of her thought, for in 1343 they had commissioned Ambrogio Lorenzetti[4] to paint the series of frescoes "Good and Bad Government" in the Palazzo Publico at Siena, the meeting place of the ministers of finance. The magistrate who is inspired by the civic ideal of good government, Catherine explains to Louis the Great, King of Hungary, "does not contaminate justice either by bowing to flattery or by wavering before threats, either to seek approval or to avoid censure; rather, he hews always to the line of justice, giving to each what reason demands."

Exemplary sovereigns, according to her, were King David and St. Louis, King of France, both of whom she said, gave to each subject what was due him, whether great or small, whether rich or poor: "they did not do as do those who reign today." She does not hesitate to criticize and she considers, in the Roman manner, that government is, above all, the observance of justice.

One idea never entered Catherine's mind — though it did the minds of the kings of France and the lords of Milan — that Catholic rulers may disregard the Church. Even though they occupy the highest posts of power, they are sons of God and spiritual subjects of the pope; they may not, therefore, exempt themselves from deference and, if need be from giving aid, to their common Father, even under the pretext that he is personally unworthy. As a son of the Church, the head of a State goes to the aid of the Pope in his hour of need, considering as done to himself the injustice done to the Pontiff and knowing that the deference paid to him is not directed to him as a mortal being but to the blood of Christ and to the authority and dignity conferred upon him by God: authority and dignity that are in no wise diminished by personal defect or guilt. And should conflict arise, temporal advantages should be disregarded until spiritual interests have been safeguarded. These are what count: when they are safeguarded temporal benefits will inevitably follow.

In the administration of kingdoms, of cities and of families Catherine castigates false charity, which is really weakness, or complicity among those responsible for the common good; she demands justice — without timidity but also without excess; she deplores indulgence toward the powerful and rigor toward the poor — defects flowing from self-love. To the senior statesmen, the consuls and the magistrates of Bologna who had sought her counsel, she wrote a long letter "with affection and love," a veritable treatise on civic and political virtues, remarking, among other things, that if "the miserable men of the world . . . recognized the truth they would see that only living in the fear of God will conserve the state and the city in peace, . . ." giving to each citizen what is his due; rendering mercy to whom mercy is due, not in sentiment but in truth; and justice to whom justice is due — tempered, however, with mercy, not made violent or bitter by anger; not through personal considerations but through zeal for the virtue itself; always attending to the common good, not to special privilege; appointing officials and administrators not out of partisan considerations, nor out of favoritism, nor from ulterior motives, much less from bribery, but exclusively according to virtue and reason. Mature men and good are to be chosen for office, not callow youths. They should be God-fearing, devoted to the common good and not to special interests. In this way they will keep their dignity and their subjects will live in peace and harmony. On the other hand, injustices, factions, the power to rule others without knowing how to rule themselves or their families — these are the concomitants of tenure by officials who are unjust or irascible, slaves of their passions and lovers of themselves; this sort of magistrate loses for society both supernatural grace and temporal well-being. Of them it may be aptly said: "Vainly the guard keeps watch, if the city has not God for its guardian" (Ps. 126:1).

It is self-love that destroys the city, whether the city of the soul or the earthly city; it is self-love that begets factions and strife. "Now this is the way," Catherine writes. "Hence I have told you that I desire to see you put off the old man and put on the new, Christ crucified: in this way you will acquire the state of grace, the secure state of your city."

Therefore in political action or in any public function whatsoever, a man in a position of authority has the duty of sanctifying himself just as has any other person: in Catherine's thought there can be no divarication — a reciprocal ignorance — between politics and religion.

From these suggestions we may form an idea of the program outlined, as if by divine intuition, as Catherine's practical application of the Gospels, in love and truth, for the art of government which, perhaps more than any other, had rebelled against the limitations and directives imposed by Christianity. In the person of His little servant, eager and animated, our Lord continued to reprove the rulers of the new Jerusalem because they persisted in playing the old political tacts instead of practicing a Christian morality which would have avoided war.

In their refractory conduct the Christians of the fourteenth century conducted themselves exactly after the manner of the Jews and pagans of the first century; they wove intricate plots, became entangled in their own webs and ended by being trapped in wars. And war weakened the authority of the Pope; it lured souls from the law of God; dissipated the finances of the communes and undermined their liberties; it worked against the common good; it weakened civilization and prepared the way for the breakup of European unity and of Christendom — in a word, it operated entirely in the service of the enemy. Catherine saw all this quite clearly: politics, by placing lies before truth, hatred before charity, became an arrogant preparation for fratricide, whose climax was the triumph of evil.

Confronted with the collapse of institutions and traditions and the very dissolution of the social order, the magistrates of the city of Florence deliberated upon a reform of their commune. An excellent idea, thought Catherine, but one which could not be effected until there were eliminated from Florentine public life the hatreds and rancors that were rife, until all those in authority were willing to give up the selfish pursuit of their own interests and work "for the common good of the whole city," and until they were disposed to renounce, if necessary, their individual opinions to concentrate upon a joint program of reform. A city cannot be ruled, or even a family, without a certain minimum of unity.

Speaking to the successor of Cardinal Albornoz[5] about his twofold duty, in the spiritual and temporal spheres, she insists that the temporal become spiritualized by the holy intention of procuring the peace and unity of the country. In a divided Christendom, Christians cut each others' throats, to the consternation of the servants of God, who are filled with bitterness, and to the exultation of the demons, "who rejoiced to see happening just what they wanted."

In this vision, simple with the simplicity of the Gospel, the relations between cliques and communes and monarchs and princelings are always relations between men, and hence subject to the laws of Christian morality. Their purpose should always be to favor, not to interfere with, good relations between governed and governing. They must be first of all Christians invested with a determined function; their mission is to know themselves, to know God, and hence to put love into practice.

Worldly-minded prelates and princelings who fancied themselves theologians sought to reconcile intrigues and the Gospel, wars and the Ten Commandments, thus separating life from the principle of life, nullifying in public life the union of human nature and divine nature in Christ, a union from which should spring the perennial Christian reconstruction of the social order. They were separating faith from works, thus destroying the effects of the Incarnation and Redemption.

Because Catherine insisted upon getting back to essentials, to the search for the kingdom of God as a necessary preliminary to realizing the kingdom of man, arrant knaves, the forerunners of Machiavelli and all who in the darkness of their sins could no longer recognize the face of a brother, dealt with her as with a fanatical, scatter-brained woman. In fact, she was quite realistic for she aimed at establishing peace through proper working conditions, through public morality, through considerations of the common good, and at placing the Pope once more in his proper position of holiness, while her opponents could not rise above fratricide, the loss of all liberty and open schism, so that an ever increasing part of Christendom was falling in ruin under the scimitar of the Turk and its own economic chaos.

Because she strove for peace and living together as brothers, to stimulate the circulation of economic goods by the concept of their belonging to God and being assigned to men as administrators of their one Father, her program seemed utopian. Because the others ruined both Church and State, dissipated the riches of culture as well as material riches, repeating mistakes that had failed a thousand times, and repeating them with unbelievable sameness and stupidity, their program seemed realistic; however, whether they knew it or not, for them reality was death.

NOTES:  Chapter 21

1. Niccolo Machiavelli, Italian political philosopher. Most famous work, *Il Principe*, containing his theory of government and maxims of "practical" statecraft.
2. "As to both Church and State, mediaeval political theory was predominantly monarchical. Ideally this flowed from the thought of God as the true monarch of the universe. Practically it comported with mediaeval social conditions. . . . The unity of the social organism is best effected by the singleness of its head. Thomas Aquinas authoritatively reasons thus, and Dante maintains that as the unifying principle is Will, the will of one man is the best means to realize it. But monarchy is no absolute right existing for the ruler's benefit; rather it is an office to be righteously exercised for the good of the community. The monarch's power is limited, and if his command outrages law or right, it is nullity; his subjects need not obey, and the principle applies that it is better to obey God than man." — Henry Osburn Taylor, *The Mediaeval Mind*, Vol. II (4th American edition), pp. 306, 307.
3. Francesco Guicciardini, political writer; died May 22, 1540.
4. A painter of the Sienese school, sometimes called Ambrogio di Lorenzo; died 1348.
5. Gil Alvarez Carillo de Albornoz, Spanish prelate and writer, Archbishop of Toledo; participated in campaigns against the Moors; to court of Pope Clement VI at Avignon; secured restoration of papal authority in Papal States.

# 22. The Writer

Catherine approached souls with a kind of hunger, she loved them so much; she saw in each one the object of the love of the Father and the redeeming blood of the Son; to each she felt herself indebted. To those to whom she could not speak she wrote. And we owe to her apostolate of the written word a nucleus of about four hundred letters (many others have been lost), in which her thought is expressed and her spirit reflected. Her more educated followers acted as her amanuenses; sometimes she dictated to them as many as four letters simultaneously, so quick was her intelligence, and so quickened were her energies by the fire of the apostolate. For example, on the morning of May 6, 1379, she dictated, in ecstasy, four letters simultaneously to four powerful rulers: to Captain Alberico da Balbiano, to Queen Giovanna of Napoli, to King Charles of France, and to the rulers of the city of Rome.

After her morning religious exercises it was Catherine's custom to go up to her room, and as she walked back and forth, to dictate letters. The words came without interruption or correction. An interior force drove her on; the apostolate gave her no pause. The amanuenses had difficulty keeping up with her dictation; sometimes they could not tell whether some particular sentence was directed at one or the other, then all three or four would write it. When they were worried about mistakes, Catherine would reassure them: "don't be disturbed, my children, this is the work of the Holy Spirit. When these letters are finished we shall see whether the sentences go together. . . ." Invariably they found that all the sentences went well in the text of each letter.

She went on dictating her letters until as she confessed to Fra Raimondo in a letter that Tommaseo[1] was to judge "of the literary excellence of the *Paradiso* of Dante, but with greater impulses of love" Providence gave her "the inclination to write." She learned to write "while sleeping," that is, in ecstasy, while she was staying at the Rocca di Tentennano, during the summer of 1377. It is not clear just how it came about. We merely know that one day while she held in her hand a pencil of red lead (used to draw miniatures) she began to transcribe these verses of a prayer which she had probably learned as a girl and had repeated many times:

> O Holy Ghost
> O Deity Eternal
> Christ-Love, come into my heart.
>
> By Thy power allure me to Thee, my God,
> and grant me charity with fear.
>
> Guard me, O Love unspeakable,
> from every evil thought;
> warm me and fire me
> with Thy sweetest love,
> that all pain may seem slight to me,
> my Holy Father, my sweet Lord.
> Help me now in my every service.
>
> Christ-Love! Christ-Love![2]

The abundance of her writing, like the abundance of her discourses, sprang from the love which impelled her to raise minds and hearts to God. "You know," she wrote to the Pope, "that the tongue speaks from a heart that overflows." Like St. Paul, her model, she spoke much and wrote much, precisely because she loved much. And she never ceased to avail herself of her secretaries, who were always happy to serve her.

The prose left to us by Catherine constitutes one of the masterpieces of Italian literature; but above all it constitutes a monument of Christian literature, although she followed no style of writing and had no artistic intention: she strove only for a divine masterpiece, the gaining of souls for Christ. If this be a defect in the eyes of aesthetic criticism it is a point of fire, a merit, an original attraction for ascetic research. Her literary style is free of any planning, the doctrine is typically hers, the method is original, elevated, and suited to the ordinary reader. In every paragraph striking imagery and unexpectedly catching phrases enliven her matter, which otherwise might appear rather uniform.

Considering the spiritual richness poured out in that prose, it would be a waste of time to try to determine how and when her thought is borrowed from others. In the prose of the *Dialogue* of which we shall speak later, an erudite person will find reminders of popular writings and stories current at that time, like paraphrases of St. Paul and St. Augustine and spiritual writers of the Middle Ages, just as, for that matter, in the discourses of our Lord related by the Evangelists there are paraphrases and reminders of the Old Testament and ways of speaking and proverbs of His own people. This detracts in no wise from Catherine's originality; as for the *Dialogue*, however, the conversation God had with her may be interpreted. Though there be phrases and manners of speaking which recall previous literature, nothing detracts from their inspired character. After all, even in the Bible God speaks the language of the people and the language of His prophets, so as to be understood by those to whom He addresses Himself. Of scholastic culture Catherine has but little; but she does have a culture that appeals to the pure of heart who love God. Our Lord had said: "He that loves me will, in turn, be loved by my Father: and I will love him, and will manifest myself to him" (Jn. 14:21); and He manifested Himself to Catherine. In this light, ornamentations of style seemed to her trickery and vanity;

and she was disgusted with those ministers of the altar "whose sermons are more to please men and strike their fancy than to give honor to God. . . . They are students not of good life but of pleasing speech," so that the faithful, as Dante complained, leave church "well fed with wind."

Catherine had certain definite truths to proclaim and she delivered herself of them just as they sprang from her spirit. She wrote just as inspiration came to her. And since she was all fire within, her prose is fiery. And this fire burns in striking purity as she closes each one of her letters: "Persevere in the sweet and holy love of God. Sweet Jesus; Jesus love." Each letter is sealed in the love of Jesus. Only in her letter to the prostitute of Perugia she adds: "Mary, sweet mother."

Surrounded by poets, among whom Pagliaresi, friend and disciple of Dante, all enamored of the beauty of nature, she willingly gave expression to the love which burned within her, and without hesitation composed verses that were effusions of her soul, such as her Christmas canticle:

> This regal Babe
> Of Bethlehem town
> Is not too small
> To wear a crown.[3]

"Like Francis of Assisi, Catherine was a jongleur of God," writes Jorgensen.

Catherine's most beautiful poetry, however, was herself; hence her followers never tired of listening to its harmony. It seemed to them a message from Paradise.

NOTES:   Chapter 22

1. Nicollo Tommaseo. Real surname, Tommašić (1802–1874). Italian writer (born in Dalmatia) and minister of public instruction. Author (with Bellini) of a dictionary of the Italian language.
2. O Spirito Santo, vieni nel mio cuore;
   per tua potenzi trailo a te, Dio vero;
   concedimi carita con timore;
   custodiscimi da ogni mal pensiero;

riscaldami e rinfiamma del tu' amore,
si che ogni peso mi paia leggero.
Santo mio Padre e dolce mio Signore,
ora aiutami in ogni mio mistiero,
Cristo amore! Cristo amore!
3. Angeluzzo picolino;
   che in Belem è nato
   non ti paia così fantino
   che gli è re incoronato.

We are grateful to Sister Madeleva, C.S.C., St. Mary's College, Notre Dame, Indiana, for these two translations.

# V. The Passion

# 23. The Crusade

Asserter of peace, protagonist of peace, Catherine accepts the Crusade, which is war. It is war directed against the infidels, but with the understanding — as Catherine explains to Messer Bartolomeo di Smeduccio, Lord of San Severino and famous soldier — that just as the Holy Sepulcher is to be freed from the infidels, the infidels in turn are to be freed from error, because "they are our brothers, redeemed as we are, by the blood of Christ." In Catherine's eyes, the ultimate justification of the "holy journey" lay in the fact that it was decreed by the Holy Father and therefore willed by God. Above all, Catherine advocated the crusade for a practical purpose — to "decongest" the body of Christendom of those passions and warlike instincts through which a people that called itself Christian, with the Pope and his prelates in the lead, squandered the resources of the Faith and of life itself to injure brothers in the Faith instead of rallying them to wrest from the infidels "that which in all reason is ours." The thought had already been expressed by Dante, whose ancestor, Cacciaguida, a soldier of the Crusade, deplores

> That ill-famed law whose folk usurp control
> To pastors' shame, of what is yours by right
> (*Paradiso*, XV, 143, 144).

So she urges all heads of states and military leaders to shed their blood for the love of Christ's Blood; she invites them to "the nuptials of everlasting life" through risk of death to recover the Holy Sepulcher. And she cannot understand how any Christian can hesitate when the Vicar of Christ is calling.

The Crusade, "the sweet and holy journey," offers each man the chance of shedding his blood for God who has given His Blood for man. Fear should not touch him, for God is with him who answers the summons of the Pope, with him who joins the side of the Omnipotent, in whose judgment death in battle is purifying martyrdom, espousal with the soul of the Lord.

At any event, even from the world political point of view, the Crusade was an urgent necessity for western Christendom, in danger of being overwhelmed by the frightening flood of the Turks. A few years before, Pietro di Cipro, after several victorious expeditions in Egypt, had been assassinated, just at the time when he was almost at the point of persuading the Christian rulers of Europe to join a combined military operation. In 1365 the Ottomans had taken Adrianople[1] by assault, to the complete consternation of Pope Urban V, at whose urging Amedeo VII of Savoia had joined the Crusade. Eminent spirits of Christendom, foreseeing the social ruin ahead because of discord prevailing among rulers and states, even in spite of the threat of the Scimitar, had begun to put the Crusade foremost in their thinking: among them was Petrarch, who for many years had made one appeal after another to the Popes at Avignon, demanding both their return to Rome and the sending of a military expedition to the Holy Land. Now, however, almost all of the Catholic rulers, swept away by the demoralizing passions of the dying Middle Ages, subordinated the Crusade to their own petty politics, and, though quite willingly they reaped the monetary advantages in the form of taxes imposed upon Church property, were quite unwilling to see any religious significance in the matter; and if they experimentally embarked upon some expedition or other, it was principally to sack the lands of infidels — and of Christians.

To reawaken the ardor of such men no one labored more than Catherine, in whose eyes the "holy journey" was a necessary phase of that rebirth of the Church, of which the restoration of the

Holy See and the reform of morals constituted the necessary fac-
tors in the re-establishment of Europe. In this peaceful rebuilding
or order — religious, political, and civil — she considered the first
step to be the rebuilding of Italy, whose fate lay close to her heart.

If, prior to this time, Catherine had been entirely oblivious of
self in her service of God, now, if possible, she thought less than
ever of herself in her single-minded service of God in His Church:
for the Church she promoted the Crusade. She writes about it to
leading political figures: to the Pope, to the Visconti, to Giovanna,
queen of Naples, to the Republic of Genoa, to Elizabeth of Poland,
mother of the king of Hungary, to Charles V of France, whom
she adjures not to dissipate the military power of France in war
with England, to Bartolomco di Smeduccio, to the Knights of
Rhodes, to Mariano d'Orsitano, governor of Sardinia, to Fra Raimondo, to Fra Guglielmo, to the great and small; at Pisa, while
devoting most of her time to this project she daringly confronted
the ferocious leader of adventurers, Giovanni Acuto. And she actually succeeded in obtaining a formal promise from him and his
followers to join the holy undertaking. This promise was explicitly
stated to Fra Raimondo whom Catherine had sent to the leader
for this purpose.

The enthusiasm which Catherine aroused was so great that
many women, perhaps wrongly interpreting some of her statements,
volunteered to take part in the expedition, to the great indignation
of don Giovanni delle Celle, who vehemently expressed his conviction that women could do no better, in this matter as in others,
than to imitate the sanctity of the Sienese tertiary, formed by eight
years of meditation, prayer, and silence.

The Crusade was proclaimed by Gregory XI in 1373; since he
had addressed himself to all the powers in Christendom, he turned
also to the weaponless Catherine, sending her a message by the
Spanish bishop Alfonso di Vadaterra, who had been the confidant
of St. Bridget. Catherine had not been acquainted with this great
woman of the North, but she knew her by reputation. She promptly
and enthusiastically responded to the Pope's appeal, not only with
the prayers which he asked for himself and for the Church, but

joyously offering her life and the lives of her followers. And she signed her reply — to signify her active apostolate — "Catherine Martha." From that moment she energetically asked businessmen and bankers to give everything, even their lives, to win back the Holy Land, for this, she assured them, was the best investment they could possibly make.

The proclamation of the Pope resounded like a reveille of spiritual renewal. Unfortunately his weakness of character — though he was a holy man — a weakness which had prompted Catherine respectfully to admonish him that he must be the strongest among high Church dignitaries, let him be persuaded to demand of the authorities at Florence, the arrest, and later, at Avignon, in March, the degrading of the leaders, real or presumed, of a revolt that had broken out: among these was Nicolo Soderini, from whom Catherine had the greatest admiration.

While this was happening, Catherine had sent the Pope another letter (the second of those that remain to us, perhaps the third that she had written), of luminous beauty, intelligent and wise, reminding the Pontiff of the cardinal law of divine economy: love, opposed by God to the whims of men; insisting that the Pope, in imitation of God Himself, should respond with mercy to the defections of Christians, for this was the only way in which he could reclaim the sheep that were lost. She asked for mercy for the accused, aligning herself with them: "We belong to you, O Father." And she assured him that there burned in all of them the desire to return to peace and communion with the Vicar of Christ. Because she saw that on the part of the Pope there was lacking in the Crusade the necessary courageous policy of making peace among Christians — without which he could not elicit all the latent moral and material support for the great undertaking — she returns again and again to this idea, as realistic as it was simple: "Raise the banner of the Holy Cross, for under that emblem you will bring about peace." Peace among Christians through war against the Mussulmans; war against the Mussulmans for peace among Christians. Hence Catherine prayed the common father of the faithful to invite his rebellious children to a holy peace, "so that the whole weight of the war could be directed against the infidels."

At Florence the orders coming from Avignon aroused consternation and more revolt, setting off a new series of antipapal conspiracies. Good men, such as Soderini, who lived under Catherine's influence, hoped to escape from that tragic dilemma of either losing their commune's liberty or rebelling against the head of the Church. And they besought her to change the mind of Gregory XI.

And Catherine could express remarkably well the sentiment of Christian people, still faithful to Christ. Others, perhaps, in her place, would have fallen either into insubordination or into adulation. Her sanctity, however, overcame such obstacles.

She stressed the desire for peace. What the people want, what the pope wants, what religion, daily work, life itself longs for is peace. And this is the basis of her program: that the Pontiff seek peace even at the cost of renouncing temporal benefits: "the treasure of the Church is the blood of Christ."

This wistful expression reveals the mentality of a woman of the people, that draws upon good sense as well as upon divine inspiration; "amid these wars and misadventures, I cannot see that you may have even one hour of well-being."

In that Guelph[2] city Catherine witnessed the results of the interdict, imposed on May 14: all the churches closed, no divine services, religious persons devoted to austere exercises of piety and works of mercy, crowds of flagellants throughout the city, over all a profound sorrow and sense of desperation. In a certain sense, it was Christ who re-entered the city; so that it became a rallying place for all those most desirous of re-establishing an accord with the Church; not a few laymen and religious became her followers.

Among these were the brothers Ristoro and Barduccio Canigiani — who became another trusted secretary of Catherine's, and the monk of Vallombroso, Giovanni delle Celle. Catherine talked with the archbishop and with the bands of the city and, after having heard their case and the reasons for their actions and at the same time having fixed the blame, in a written document, for the revolt against the Pope, she acceded to their prayer to carry the cause of the Florentines to the court of Avignon itself. For this purpose she announced her coming immediately to Pope Gregory XI so as to predispose him to pardon and to beg him not to dispatch the troops he had already enrolled for the purpose.

Fragile though she was, she set out for Avignon, accompanied by twenty-three followers — Dominican friars and nuns as well as laymen. She stopped at Bologna to pray at the tomb of "that Spaniard" who was her spiritual father, St. Dominic. She reached Avignon on the evening of August 18, after more than twenty days of travel. From aboard her ship which slowly ascended the Rhone she could contemplate the little French town which had become the new Babylon, within whose walls arose the Gothic mass of the pontifical palace, resembling a fortress, all towers and bastions.

A Pope endowed with her heart and her fortitude would certainly have initiated the reform of the Church, would have brought about peace, at least in Italy, and would have returned to his See in Rome; thus in that critical hour he would have re-established the pre-eminence of the spirit. What was lacking was holiness: Catherine could accomplish much, but, after all, she was a simple nun.

So far away was peace among Christians that on March 20, Bologna, up to then the most faithful of the papal domains, forcibly expelled the Cardinal of Sant' Angelo and proclaimed itself an independent republic. Eight days later Acuto occupied Faenza, where, to the cry of "Long live the Church!" he ordered his mercenaries to slay the men and rape the women of the town.

In a frenzy of political fury, abandoning his timid aspirations for the Crusade and for peace, Gregory XI was merely annoyed with himself for not having humiliated Florence; forthwith he proclaimed an interdict upon the republic, excommunicating its leading citizens, among them Soderini.

NOTES: Chapter 23

1. The Turkish Edirne, northwest of Constantinople.
2. The Guelph party in Mediaeval Italy was papal and popular, as opposed to the Ghibelline party, imperial and aristocratic.

## 24. At Avignon

The interdict had fallen like a bomb upon the Christian populace of Florence. Deprived of the privileges of public worship, the Mass, the sacraments, Christian burial, Florence was like a doomed city within its walls, inhabited in the midst of its splendid churches by the spirits of the damned. The spectacle terrified its citizens, exposed to the wrath of God and of men, for the effects of the interdict extended beyond religion into politics and economics, so that the excommunicated lost not only their temporal goods but all their rights, became outlaws in the eyes of Christendom, no longer capable of making contracts or expecting pacts to be observed, liable to be reduced to slavery and considered proper objects of war without quarter. For the Florentines the interdict meant a mortal blow to their banking and commercial interests; their debtors from outside promptly refused to repay, seized the goods and, when possible, even the persons of their creditors.

In the face of utter collapse, serious men, like Soderini and other leaders in Florence, turned to Catherine, pleading with her to intervene with the Pope. Catherine was the one person who, while she shared intimately the anxieties of the people and their apprehension for the misdeeds of the Pope's legates, preserved intact her reverence for the keys of Peter and hence was esteemed both at Florence and at Avignon. For holiness, constancy, and longsightedness no one else so well as she was in a position to accomplish that mission of reconciliation which by the divine Master has really been committed to each of His followers. For love of Christ and of His people Catherine undertook the task. In customary fashion she devoted herself entirely to the work, determined not to be stopped by any obstacle, even unto death. And she yearned for death because to shed her blood for Christ, to become a martyr, would be the crowning of all her efforts.

As a first step she sent one of her most remarkable letters to the Pope at Avignon, entrusting it to the hands of those "true servants of God," the faithful friars Raimondo, Giovanni Tantucci, Felice da Massa, and other companions, who set out, as she wrote, "representing Christ crucified and me."

In the letter, therefore, Christ speaks. She begins with an augury of abundant grace for the Pope so that he may become the instrument and cause of universal peace; and he will become so if he will, with virile soul, set about the accomplishment of three projects:

1. The reform of the Church, with the elimination of unworthy pastors who, instead of being fathers of the poor are interested only in accumulating wealth, plundering, and scandalizing the faithful;

2. The return of the successor of Peter to his See in Rome, to be effected not by force of arms but through the force of love in the footsteps of the immolated Lamb;

3. The Crusade, to free Christians from war and infidels from unbelief.

This is the mandate that Christ and Catherine confide to the Pope by the hands of the servants of God, instructed to elaborate upon the points before the papal Curia.

So that their spirit would be maintained continually upon a supernatural plane of charity, even in that ambient of flatteries and scandals, Catherine tells them of an encounter she has had with our Lord. Nothing strengthens the faith of her followers so much as a knowledge of the mystical life of their spiritual mother — from which they themselves live, growing in God through her. She tells them, therefore, how on the night of April 2 of that year (1376) her soul, as if separated from her body, beheld in God's light the mystery of the current persecutions of the Church and of its imminent reform and exaltation. In the vision God had shown her that of necessity scandals would come but that He would intervene to cleanse the profaned Church, just as He had, with whip in hand, cleansed the temple, not wishing the house of prayer to become a den of thieves. Then her soul in ecstasy had seen enter the side of Christ the two peoples now adversaries — Christian and infidel — while she, as mediatrix, passed among them, accompanied by St. Dominic, Fra Raimondo, and all her followers.

Her soul, immersed in joy, understood that the triumph of the Church would follow her tribulations, brought on by wicked Christians; and at the sight of that transformation, she found herself whispering the *Nunc dimittis*. . . .

> Now you may release
> your bondsman, O Master,
> according to your promise,
> in peace!
> For my eyes have looked upon the salvation
> which you have prepared
> for all the nations to behold . . .
> (Lk. 2:29–31).

In the future, therefore, she sees the dawn of the emancipation of the Church from her present miseries; and this provision must have been great comfort for her spiritual sons who, in turn, were able to send her comforting news from Avignon; while at Florence the hope was expressed that Catherine would come there from Siena the more easily at the scene of action to bring to a happy conclusion her work of peacemaking. She took up the suggestion; with Stefano Maconi, a recent convert, and his friend, Neri di Landuccio and Fra Bartolomeo Dominici, she set out for Florence, where she was received at the city gate by all the heads of the corporations[1] and conducted to the Bishop's palace to be the guest there of Archbishop Angelo Ricasoli.

NOTE: *Chapter 24*

1. There were voluntary organizations of those who exercised the same trade or profession. Their functions were economic, political, judiciary, assistential, and religious.

## 25. At the Papal Court

At Avignon Catherine encountered painters from Siena and bankers from Florence; but the sight that brought most smiles to her face was that of Fra Raimondo and her other spiritual sons. With them she was housed in a Cardinal's palace and after two days was granted an audience by the Pope. The encounter was dramatic — a sovereign pontiff seated on his throne, and a humble nun, on her knees before him, along with Fra Raimondo who acted as interpreter. The Pope, although barely forty-five years of age, seemed quite aged under the weight of the tremendous difficulties in which he found himself, his mind vacillating between good intentions and traditions of nepotism. He had labored so hard to reconcile the French and the English, the Castilians and the Kingdom of Aragon, the Greeks and the Latins; yet he realized that from his very court had erupted the motives of conflict, among the worst that of proud Florence and that of cruel Milan.

An indication of the fundamental goodness of his soul was this: for some time, and repeatedly, he had sought Catherine's counsels and her prayers; he was evidently impressed by her wisdom, her realistic approach, her reverence and, most of all, by her holiness. Now seeing her face to face, humble, unassuming, her eyes shining with an inner light, he was glad of the opportunity to learn her thoughts more directly; he listened to her with fatherly interest. Upon learning of the Florentines' desire for peace he was overjoyed and he brought their rather lengthy conversation to a close by declaring himself disposed and happy to receive the Florentines again as sons and leaving to Catherine to work out the details as seemed best to her. He did not go more into detail for he was expecting the regular ambassadors from Florence.

Poor Catherine! After just one week, writing to Florence to the "Eight of War," called wryly by their followers in an attempt at praise, the "Eight Saints," she was constrained to tell them, politely, of her disappointment with their actions, for although their words were peaceful, their acts were not. In her absence they had gone so far as to impose taxes upon Church property and to take other similar measures hardly designed to promote accord with the Pope: after this sort of double dealing she feared condemnation for the Florentines and shame for herself. And her presentiment was justified; when the Florentine ambassadors arrived at Avignon they would have nothing to do with Catherine; representatives of a new city government, created on July 6, they had come only to gain time and not to make peace. They had decided to trifle with the Pontiff and the saints, adroitly playing the protagonists of war against the partisans of peace in what was later seen to be the best manner of Machiavelli.

Catherine was disconcerted, but she did not give up. She concentrated her forces upon the central problems of the complex crisis from which Christendom was suffering, working all the harder now that she knew she had the support and blessing of "the sweet Christ upon earth," His Vicar.

First of all, the reform of morals in ecclesiastical circles. Avignon, in the eyes of all Christians, from Petrarch to Cola di Rienzo, from Chaucer to Peter of Aragon, was the hotbed of clerical decadence. Catherine went the rounds of that court somewhat after the manner of Jesus in the temple. She had profound filial devotion for the Pope, "sweet Christ on earth," and just by using this title she professed her faith as a secure and understanding Catholic; but at the same time she spoke the truth, pointing out to the Pontiff errors and abuses that were rampant; she fought simony; she castigated vice. At certain times she seemed to be purity itself in the midst of corruption, innocence in the midst of sin, the true likeness of the Church, virgin and mother, confronting an Anti-Church bedecked in pontifical robes. Women of easy virtue whom she encountered in the salons of Avignon looked her over with curiosity and hostility; functionaries were annoyed by the presence of a creature who insisted upon the code of a past era; cardinals could hardly conceal their apprehensive disdain. In an audience with the Pope, at which Fra Raimondo translated her Tuscan idiom into Latin, Catherine lamented that at the Roman Curia instead of finding a paradise of heavenly virtues she had come upon a sink of infernal vices. "How can it be," the Pontiff, moved and saddened, asked her, "that in these few days you have been able so well to recognize the morals of the Roman Curia?" Humbly, Catherine rose to her feet and in an attitude of majesty, her eyes flashing, she exclaimed: "For the honor of Almighty God I dare to say that even while in my native Siena I have smelled a greater stench of sins committed at the Roman Curia than those perceive who have committed and are committing them every day." The Pope was silent and the interpreter, pale and embarrassed asked her by what authority she dared so to speak.

It was love that made her speak; it was truth that made her take this liberty. Because she loved Christ, Catherine loved his Vicar, Christ upon earth; and this in an epoch when, as a citizen of Siena, she had to be tenaciously Ghibelline, and as a Tuscan, she had to remember the specter of antipapal Florence, and as an Italian she had to think of Rome, of Milan and of other centers of disorder and rebellion; in an epoch in which even Catholic nations made war upon the Pope, so that half of Christendom was in revolt against the Holy See, and an anticlerical literature made abominable charges against the court at Avignon; in an epoch, above all, in which the Pope made little effort to be loved and did much to be feared and even hated, while the Turk assembled his destroying hordes against the name of Christ. But for Catherine the Pope represented the hinge upon which the collective life of Christian peoples must turn; and if this hinge was broken, social order would collapse. The Pope might even be the devil incarnate; but he was the Pope, the basis of universal peace. And if sin touched him that was no justification for the sin of Christians who rebelled against him. Sons never have sufficient reason to rebel against their father, nor Christians to rebel against the Pope.

Catherine is the herald of the Holy See; she is the voice of the Church militant in defense of the clergy and of him who is at their head. She castigates personal defects, evil public conduct, but she always holds inviolate the divine title of their dignity. She stands before the Pontiff as a daughter before her father. From her words — now suave, now burning — she shows that the honor and the office of the Papacy are as close to her heart as the honor of God and of His Church. And because her words are an expression of God's will she is able, with her love that is stronger than death, to give counsel, advice, even commands, to the Pope, speaking in the name of Christ in heaven to His vicar on earth; and the Pope listens to her and humbly asks her blessing.

Thus she succeeds in recreating faith in the papacy; and she recreates it in the Pope himself, in whom, at the lax court of Avignon, that faith and confidence were waning. That worldliness had lasted a long time now, its evil aggravated with the generations. Dante had raised his scornful voice to protest the decadence of the papal curia:

"Where every day the Christ is bought and sold" and Petrarch, too, who thus pictures the court of Avignon:

> "Within your chambers young girls and old men
> Are flirting, and the devil in the middle
> With bellows, mirrors, fire, prepares his riddle."
>
> (Sonnet CXXXVI)

Hence Dante had also urged the return of Peter to his proper See. Cola di Rienzo[1] and frequent legations from the city of Peter had also urged the Pope's return, for at Rome, in the absence of her Supreme Shepherd, the most glorious monuments of Christendom, basilicas and sanctuaries, were little by little falling into ruins, amidst universal desolation. Blessed Colombini likewise had deplored the decadence of religion: "Look around you at the things of Christ; His name is preached and sung every day, but how is He treated? . . . He has been driven out of every religious house." For his part, Colombini preferred to seek converts among the taverns rather than among simonical and corrupt religious, deaf to every counsel of holiness.

Catherine, however, wished to convert all — large and small, those in high places and those in low, for evil had infected both head and members. Because she loved Christ, because she loved the Pope, she loved also the Church, the Mystical Christ, whose sufferings supply what is lacking in the sufferings of Christ upon the cross (Coloss. 1:24). The Church "is Christ Himself and she dispenses the sacraments and gives us life." Hence to rebel against the Church is to become cut off from its life, with withered members of a body; it is to expose one's self to eternal death. True, in many of her members the Church appears corrupt, and Catherine does not hesitate to condemn them. But she is careful to point out, in every circumstance and with all clarity, that the divine virtue and the force of the Church remain intact. She considers these evils to be her own personally, and speaking of them to a prelate she exclaims: "Alas, alas, how miserable is my soul!"

Christendom seems to her as a flock attacked by wolves, while the shepherds sleep in their self-love, their pride, their cupidity, whence they even stoop to simony, to trafficking in the gifts and graces of God. She always mentions self-love first, as being the origin of all vices just as love of God is the origin of all virtues. The former renders prelates servile; the latter can make them virile of heart, capable of speaking the truth and of acting according to justice.

NOTE: Chapter 25

1. Real name: Niccolo Gabrini, Italian patriot, called "Last of the Romans"; murdered October 8, 1354.

## 26. The Pope's Return to Rome

"Arise, then, Holy Father — no more negligence! . . . Come, come, to console the servants of God and your sons. We await you with affectionate and breathless desire."

Thus Catherine wrote to the Pontiff toward the end of 1375, begging him to come back to Rome. Just as too many bishops resided away from their episcopal sees, so that the episcopal duty of the apostolate had become for them merely a source of income, so the Bishop of Rome lived away from his See, at Avignon: and this was a major factor in the universal disorder that prevailed.

Exhorted by good men and solicited by events themselves, Gregory XI sensed that his return to the Apostolic See at Rome could no longer be put off; and on January 6, 1376, a few days after the receipt of Catherine's letter, he addressed a message to the Christian world announcing his proposal to betake himself to the See of Peter and to live and die among the Romans.

Then the rebellion of Tuscany and of Emilia, besides that of the Duchy of Milan, seemed to put an end to the Pope's generous decision, to the satisfaction of the swarm of French cardinals and the courtiers and courtesans of Avignon. The cardinals — twenty-six in all, of whom one was Spanish, four Italian, and the others French

176

— reminded the Pope of the precedent set by Clement IV, who, before deciding to leave Avignon, had asked the consent of the sacred college. But the sacred college, composed mostly of Frenchmen, was not at all attracted by the idea of leaving their comforts on the banks of the Rhone, under the protection of the King of France, for the hazards of the City on the banks of the Tiber, at the mercy of marauding noblemen and common brigands. Whereupon Catherine, in a letter to the Pope, opposed to the example of Clement that of Urban V, who had not sought counsel from anyone when there was question of a thing certain and manifest, such as the return of the Holy See to Rome. And she suggested to him a "holy deceit": to pretend that he was postponing his return until later on while actually starting out as soon as possible. Fra Raimondo translated the letter into Latin; the Pope did as Catherine suggested.

The cardinals of the opposition were simply spokesmen of the French monarch which, having sealed off the Holy See within its realm, had no intention of letting it escape, now that it could help in establishing French domination over all Christendom.

But Catherine was a troublesome obstacle in the way of such design. Everybody at the court was talking about her. The ladies of the court of Avignon who had, without effect, used their gossip, their flattery and their wiles upon the young woman from Siena, who from their jeweled and perfumed bodies had experienced the stench of their sins and more than once had rebuffed them in holy anger, now circulated throughout France the wildest tales about the moral influence of this young woman upon the weak Pope. These rumors were taken up by unscrupulous members of the clergy, some of whom, even at Avignon, had attempted to catch her in heresy, by syllogizing captiously about the ecstasies and fastings of her whom they depicted as a cheap, silly woman. The royal court at Paris was so much concerned about the turn of events that the brother of the King, the duke of Anjou, was dispatched to Avignon to confront Catherine and get rid of her. The duke did confront her; but he was converted by her to the cause of the crusade. He actually promised to enroll an armed force, and he begged her to write to the king. So Catherine wrote to the king, as to her "dear lord and father," to persuade him, too, to become a follower of the Cross, ready to accept sufferings and abuse and renunciation as gifts of the divine goodness. For Catherine loved in King Charles V as she loved in the tailor, Francesco di Pipino, a soul redeemed by the blood of Christ. She thus interpreted for him the duties of his royal state:

1. To consider his power as a loan from God and not as his own property. Thus she struck at the roots of the then fashionable jurisdictional theory by which legalists and hired theologians were building up an absolute monarchy of divine right. The sovereign who claims as his own the power that comes from God behaves as a robber and a fool. Since Charles V is called the Wise, let him show his wisdom by using his power in the way God has entrusted it to him.

2. To consider riches also as given by God to be used for the benefit of the poor; hence not to amass riches or use economic power against those economically weak; rather to recognize the moral law in economic life, punishing wrongdoing and rewarding virtue with firm-handed justice.

3. To do what Catherine most desired in a sovereign: to love his fellow men rather than to make war upon them. If in carrying out this vital precept the king must lose his wealth or even his life, let him do so willingly: what is important is the soul. With the elimination of wars, the way will be cleared for "the mystery of the holy journey," the crusade.

Everything is reduced to love, the only thing that matters.

Calmly and serenely she concludes: "Your Majesty should be ashamed of the obstacles put in the way of the crusade — you and other Christian lords. This is a grave scandal before men and an abomination before God that war should be made upon brothers while the enemy is left unmolested; that you desire to take from others what belongs to them rather than reacquire what is rightly yours. . . . I tell you, in the name of Christ crucified, that you may no longer delay in making this peace. Make peace; and confine your warmaking to the infidels. . . ."

Catherine also turns again to the brother of the king, exhorting him to make the crusade without further loss of time, to start moving even before the Pontiff departs from Avignon. And with keen intuition she also proposes to the Pope that he seek a leader for the crusade. She is consumed with the desire for quick action; she knows how short is the time and how urgent it is to make use of it as God wills.

To deter the Pope, the French cardinals and the courtiers exaggerate the risks of the venture, even warning him of the likelihood of attempts to poison him or assassinate him on the trip to Rome; as a matter of fact, the Florentines, instead of obeying Catherine, were hatching a plot among the states of Italy and outside Italy against the Holy See, to destroy or at least weaken the temporal power of the papacy in Italy. But Catherine does not hesitate, nor does she waver in her plan, although word of the proposed poisoning is communicated to the Pope in a letter from a holy man, the Franciscan Pietro d'Aragon, or at least in his name.

Shrewdly Catherine suspects that this letter is a forgery by someone right there in the papal court, over the name of a holy friar. She exhorts the Pope to be a man and not a child and points out to him that poison can be administered at Avignon as well as at Rome; indeed had not Pope Urban been poisoned at Avignon, after his return from Rome?

With words of fire, now more than ever convinced that she speaks the will of God, Catherine breaks the Pope's indecision and — alone — defeats the whole crowd of the opposition, representing the top leaders in the Church and in the Papal States. United to the Crucified, with Him she conquers the world. And because, like Him, she is all love, she knows no fear — the fear that is born only where love dies.

This was the most heroic and most arduous undertaking of her life. To it she summoned all the power of her will and the weight of her prestige. In those days she struck holy terror in those whose conscience bothered them: divine vengeance seemed to go out from her. And she herself sensed that her adversaries — demons and their exponents — hard pressed by evidence of the divine will, finally were giving up. Writing to her mother a little later on, during her return trip, she recalled that her mission to Avignon was willed by God and not by men, that there was something mysterious about its success and that it had been concluded "not without beneficial results."

The most beneficial result for the Christian world was that the Pope set out for Marseille to embark for Rome on September 13. That day marked the end of the exile at Avignon, which had lasted for seventy years. It marked one of the most important events of history, freighted with consequence — an event which for centuries has been discussed by students of history and politics, has been the subject of writers and artists. The hand of a simple virgin had removed barriers that seemed immovable, had done what neither writers nor diplomats nor rulers had been able to do.

The same day Catherine left with her party for Toulon whence, to escape the applause of the archbishop and his people she decided to travel by sea. Sailing along the coast of the Ligurian Sea, the caravan arrived on October 3 at Varazze, where she was happy to visit the birthplace of Blessed Jacopo, author of the *Leggenda Aurea*, from which, as a child, she had caught her first glimpse of holiness. She proposed to the citizens that they erect a church in his honor, to be freed from the plague. They did so and obtained the favor.

At Genoa she and her companions were guests of the Scotti family, in whose palace they remained much longer than anticipated for the reason that Neri fell ill and Maconi, Tantucci, and Fra Dominici, exhausted by the rigors of travel and perhaps suffering from an infection contracted at Varazze, had to rest.

Catherine's absence had grieved her parents. Monna Lapa could not yet reconcile herself to the idea that her daughter now belonged to God and not to the Benincasa family. Catherine begged her to remember the example of Mary and not to consider herself abandoned. Perhaps in her conversations with Lapa, Giovanna di Corrado, mother of Maconi, also complained that Catherine had taken away her son, Stefano; for Giovanna, too, loved her child with a too sensitive affection. Both forgot the Christ's precept: He who is fonder of father or mother than of me is not worthy of me; and he who is fonder of son or daughter than of me is not worthy of me. And he who will not shoulder his cross and follow me is not worthy of me (Mt. 10:37, 38). Catherine reminds Giovanna and her husband of this truth, points out that theirs must be a joyous offering of their son to God. And the worthy mother of that generous son accepts — at least in a first gesture of dedication — this difficult teaching and becomes herself a disciple of Catherine who now, in writing to her, may call her sister and daughter and explain to her that sons as well as other created things must be loved for love of Him.

This intervention of Catherine in the attitude of parents reveals the manner in which she herself loved those who became her followers. She loved them in God. This does not mean, however, that her love extended only to the spirit. Formed on that human-divine love of the Man-God, she loved each person in God but entirely. So, as Neri was gravely ill by now, she cast herself down to pray to her divine Spouse as was her custom in graver cases, saying to Him: "I wish him to be cured." And to Maconi — less seriously ill — she simply says: "I wish absolutely that you get well . . . in the name of holy obedience, get well!" Both recovered.

An indication of the reciprocal love that existed among them was the fact that Stefano induced Catherine to intercede for Neri — Stefano on his knees before her, weeping, asking her intervention so that the voyage undertaken for the love of God and their spiritual mother would not be marred by the death of a companion and brother "in a foreign land."

Catherine spent these days at Genoa visiting monasteries and writing letters; she was tireless, burning and consumed by her thirst for souls. Even in her quarters, her resourcefulness kept her continually occupied: there she received humble artisans, sailors, doctors of theology, jurisconsults, government officials, greeting each one with her dazzling smile that was like God's stamp of approval. In that light her hearers — perhaps for the first time in their lives — invariably were impelled to speak the whole truth, in a spirit of charity which made it more sharp and burning.

One evening, without any announcement, the Pope himself came to see her. After disembarking he was physically and morally exhausted. The voyage with the sumptuous papal fleet, escorted by ships belonging to friendly powers, had not been a pleasure trip; violent storms had buffeted the flotilla from one port to another, while atrocious doubts and hot tempered insinuations had attacked his wavering soul, convincing him that the venture of returning to Rome upon which he had embarked was too much for human powers. And perhaps it was. At any rate, in this state of mind he sought out Catherine. Weeping, he had already sought the advice of his cardinals and the French cardinals had replied to him: "You see, even the elements are against us!" And they were quick to tell him that in those very days an insurrection had broken out at Rome, while the Florentines had embarked upon a victorious war against the pontifical troops. Hence — this was the advice of the majority — nothing remained but to return to the tranquillity of Provence, to Avignon. And he was about to turn back; but in his mind there had been one fixed thought: he must talk again to Catherine.

He must listen to her again: for she would know how to restore his confidence and show him the will of God. However, the cardinals would certainly have objected to having that little Dominican tertiary, a slender shadow in white and black, pass silently through the corridors of the papal court, prepared to spoil all their plans. So Gregory XI furtively betook himself, just as darkness was falling, to the home of the Scotti, in search of Catherine.

He was dressed as a simple priest and he was thoroughly depressed. At the sight of him Catherine dropped to her knees, but the Pope raised her up and indicated that he wished to talk to her. The conversation lasted until late that night. Returning to his cardinals, Gregory XI was a changed man. Catherine's words had "edified and strengthened" him, giving him the energy necessary to take up the trip once more to its destination. On October 29 he set sail again. Arriving at Livorno he was royally greeted by the head of the commune, an ardent admirer of Catherine, Piero Gambacorti. Thence he traveled to Corneto, in the Papal States, where he arrived on December 5. There he received another letter from Catherine, in which she reasserted the motives of the peace: for the glory of God, the reform of the Church, and the happy conclusion of the Pope's journey. As a matter of fact during the Pope's whole trip Catherine had been in touch with him to sustain him by her exhortations. She felt terribly alone and helpless in her struggle against the whole devilish system of money, of ambition, of worldly power; yet she sustained the attack with tranquil vigor, relying upon the cross to have God with her. During each night, spent mostly in prayer, she wrote out her saddened pleas, her arguments, humble yet insistent, that the Pope would carry out his project without fear of the difficulties that abounded. Inspired by her courage and indomitable will, the Pontiff won the day.

"If his (the Pope's) hesitancy displeases Thee, O God of love" — she prayed — "punish my own body, which I offer Thee, to be scourged and destroyed according to Thy pleasure." The last letter from Catherine during the Pope's sojourn at Corneto came from Pisa, where Lapa, eager to see her daughter again, Fra Tommaso, and numerous other followers had gathered to greet Catherine. And from Pisa, with that loving sensitiveness that looked out for everyone's happiness, Catherine sent Stefano to his mother at Siena. Stefano, who was closely united to his spiritual mother and through her to all her followers, no sooner had left them than he felt the stabbing emptiness of separation. When creatures are of one heart and one mind separation becomes part of the passion and death of Christ, prolonged in His Mystical Body; Stefano, not daring, out of reverence, to write directly to Catherine, tells his sadness to Neri, saying that he can hardly wait until she reaches Siena and that he regrets having left the group. "For now I can write no more, only that you embrace our sweet mother for me and tell her what I have written. Remember me to my fathers, Fra Raimondo, Brother Maestro (Giovanni Tantucci), Fra Bartolomeo, and Fra Felice, and embrace Lapa for me, asking them to pray for me . . . God knows how unhappy I am! If it were not for the hope of seeing you soon . . . I know not what I should do. . . ."

Meanwhile the Pope prepared to leave Corneto for Rome, where rival factions were tearing each other to pieces, ready, however, at any moment to join forces against the Pontiff. Finally, however, on December 21, the city submitted and on January 17, 1377, the Supreme Pontiff, having arrived at Ostia, made solemn entrance into the city through the Porta San Paolo, riding a white mule, showered with confetti and flowers, amidst the delirious acclamations of the populace. The reception was so enthusiastic and spontaneous and colorful that the observant papal librarian, Pierre Ameilh, who was then compiling a poetic *Itinerarium Gregorii XI*[1] was much impressed: "Truly I should never have expected, in our time, to see with my own eyes such glory."

It was truly the Catholic soul of the people that exploded in joy, rising above the factions of the Colonna and the Savelli and calling back to the city many of the bourgeoisie who had fled.

At last the tragic interval was ended: her "sweet father" had returned to his home and Catherine, on her knees, besought the Lord that because of his sins other disorders might not afflict the body of the Church.

The reinstatement of the papacy in its rightful place was not only an event, important though it was, in the history of the popes: it was an act that sent new energies flowing through the body of the Church. It was a renascence with consequences that were religious, moral, and political, with effects that were universal. With it began the second part of Catherine's program: the renascence of the Church through the reforms of its pastors. Many bishops, following the example of the Bishop of Rome, returned to their sees, too long vacant. The choice of cardinals and bishops was taken out of French politics and the papacy was liberated from vassalage to the French crown. The City of Rome, with its monuments both sacred and profane, with its relics and its landmarks, began to recover its vigor, despite turbulent and murderous factions, and to become once more the goal of pilgrimages and the common center of peoples: not the least evidence of that reawakening of Catholicism, to which Catherine had given a decisive stimulus.

NOTE:  Chapter 26

1. Literally, "The Travels of Gregory XI."

VI. *Death*

## 27. Catherine at Florence

Catherine did not rest. The Pope at Rome had now to confront the first difficulties of governing a community where, as almost everywhere else, the common people had gained the advantage over the Roman aristocracy and with a city government of thirteen representatives of the thirteen *rioni* or wards had rendered impotent the power of a senator. Catherine bade the Pope not to rest at restoring civil order but to proceed with all the energy he could muster to a reform of the Church. As usual, she was radical. She wrote to the Pope: "Offer your life for Christ crucified; uproot vice, encourage the practice of virtue." And if he did not feel up to such action, let him entrust the high responsibility to someone else.

For her part she kept working at Siena on the arduous task — a veritable labor of Sisyphus[1] — of reconciling the Florentines with the Pope. At her urging the Pontiff, while still as Corneto, had invited the Florentine republic to send ambassadors to him at Rome. And indeed Florentine ambassadors did come to Rome, but to conduct themselves as they had at Avignon — masterful inactivity, so as not to reach any agreement. Once more Catherine encountered imposing obstacles conjured up by both sides: on the one hand, the Florentines were preparing war because they trusted in armed might; on the other hand, the Pope was similarly engaged because, although he had confidence in Catherine's prayers, he really relied — or he was so compelled by worldly-minded cardinals — upon bands of adventurers whose command he had entrusted to the worldly and intriguing cardinal, Roberto di Ginevra, a future anti-pope.

At the command of the lame cardinal the Bretons one day perpetuated the infamous slaughter of Cesena. Because the citizens of that town, determined to endure no longer the vexations of the undisciplined mercenaries, rebelled, and, in the street fighting that ensued, had killed more than three hundred Bretons, the cardinal summoned the villainous forces of Acuto, ordering them to inflict thorough punishment upon the city, now unarmed by a deceitful promise of the cardinal himself. The bandits, falling upon a helpless populace, put to the sword all the citizens who had not managed to flee, hence all the aged, children and women, making no distinction between lay persons and religious, after raping nuns and other women, sacking and robbing sanctuaries and homes. And all in the name of Holy Church!

In the face of this slaughter, the leaders of Florence, the so-called "Eight of War," for whom the return of the Pope had destroyed a pretext of expanding the dominion of the Republic into the papal states, found a new argument for warlike preparations, justifying themselves in the eyes of the people, who were opposed to war (of this Fra Raimondo was convinced by his own experiences), and abandoning themselves to other provocative acts such as actually hiring the mercenaries of Acuto, who had just finished the massacre of Cesena and like all other bands of venal assassins sold themselves to the highest bidder, Determined to wage war, the "Eight Saints" declared open war upon the Church itself, as such, declaring an end to the interdict, which had now lasted seventeen months, and ordering the resumption of religious services, threatening heavy fines upon churchmen who would not co-operate.

While these events were transpiring at Florence and at Rome, Catherine had taken up again her apostolate at Siena. Among her accomplishments there was the opening of a new convent for her sisters, called Santa Maria degli Angeli, rebuilt from the castle of Belcaro which had been given to her by a noble convert, Nanni di Vanni Savini. He had been a violent youth, haughty and boastful, a typical figure of the times when too many men lived upon — or died from — factional hatred and strife. He had been recommended to Catherine by the Augustinian, Guglielmo Flete. Although he had been deaf to the pleadings of two esteemed and learned directors of conscience, Fra Guglielmo and Fra Raimondo, he capitulated to Catherine; kneeling at her feet he promised to mend his ways and to be reconciled with every one of his enemies.

Another conversion, perhaps the most dramatic of all and most characteristic of Catherine's work, was that of the young Nicolò Toldo, condemned to death for having spoken ill of the Republic. He was a nobleman of Perugia, whose character and family background had given promise of a splendid future. He was in the dirty jail, awaiting decapitation like a common assassin when the priest, Tommaso Caffarini, came to speak to him of resignation. He turned upon Caffarini furiously, blaspheming against a God who permitted such savagery. The case was desperate. Catherine was asked to visit the young man in his cell. No one else could relate what followed so well as the saint herself, as she did in a letter dictated to Fra Raimondo: "I had already received a suggestion as how to proceed — a suggestion of such charm that the heart cannot think of it nor tongue speak, nor eye see, nor ear hear. The will of God, among His other mysteries, preceded me; it would take too much time to explain. I went to visit him whom you know: he received such comfort and consolation that he was completely resigned, and went to confession. And he made me promise, by God's love, that when his time would come I should be with him. I promised and I was there. I went to him early that fateful morning and he received great consolation. He assisted at Mass and received Holy Communion — his first. His will was attuned to the will of God and subject to it; there remained only a certain apprenhension lest he would not be strong enough at the very end. However, the immeasurable and burning goodness of God was his strength, inspiring him with such affection and love in the desire for God that he kept repeating: 'Abide with me and do not abandon me!' And I held his head on my breast and I sensed his happiness, a new odor in his blood; and it was like the odor of mine as I long to shed it for Jesus, my Spouse. And as this desire grew in my soul I sensed a touch of fear in him and I said: 'Take comfort, my sweet brother; for soon we shall be admitted to the espousals. You will be bathed in the sweet blood of the Son of God, our adored Jesus, Whom I want you to keep ever before your mind. And I shall await you at the place of justice. Take heed, then, my son, that you banish every fear from your heart; let your countenance change sadness into joy!' And he was happy and exclaimed in exultation: 'Whence should such grace be mine, that my sweet friend will be waiting for me in the holy place of justice?' You see that he had been filled with such light that he called *holy* the place of justice! Then he said: 'I shall go forth all strong and glorious; it will seem a thousands years before I reach there, thinking all the while that you will be waiting for me.' And he spoke words so sweet that they must have come straight from the goodness of God.

"So I waited for him at the place of execution; and as I waited I prayed earnestly in the presence of Mary and Catherine, virgin and martyr. But before reaching him I knelt down and placed my own neck on the executioner's block; but I was filled with revulsion — I was too filled with self-love. I rose and I prayed again and exclaimed: 'Mary! I wish this favor, that right up to the time of his execution he will have interior light and peace of heart so that I may see him strong to the last.' Then my soul was filled with consolation so that, although there was a crowd around I could not see anyone for happiness at the promise he had made me.

"Then he came, meek as a lamb, and seeing me he began to smile; and he turned to indicate that I was to make the sign of the cross over him. When I had done so I said 'Kneel down! to the nuptials, my sweet brother! Soon you will be enjoying eternal life.' He knelt down with great meekness; and bending over him I laid bare his neck and reminded him of the blood of the Lamb. His lips kept murmuring 'Jesus!' . . . then, 'Catherine!' As he spoke my name I took his head between my hands, reminding him of the goodness of God and I said to him: 'I wish it!' — Then the God-Man appeared, as if in the brightness of the noon-day sun; He appeared distinctly and received Nicolò's blood; in that blood there was the fire of holy longing, given to him and hidden in his soul through grace; Our Lord received it into the fire of His own divine love. Because He had received the blood and fulfilled the youth's desire, He received his soul and mercifully placed it in the wound in His side. Truth Itself manifested that He received that soul by His grace and His mercy and not through any human merit. O how sweet and ineffable to see the goodness of God! With what tenderness and love He watched that soul as it left the body!" . . . "Nicolò had behaved with such charm as to attract a thousand hearts. And I was not surprised, because he was already tasting the sweetness of God. He turned slightly, as a bride would when she is about to meet her bridegroom, turning her eyes and her head and bowing her thanks to those who have accompanied her.

"Seeing that gesture, my soul, reposed in peace and quiet, though I was faint at sight of the blood that covered him. Oh, how miserable I am! I cannot say more. I remained upon the ground, envying him. Do not wonder, then, that I urge nothing more upon you than that you be nourished in the blood and the fire that come from the side of the Son of God. Delay no longer, my dearest children, for the blood is flowing and will give you life. My sweet Jesus; Jesus, my love."

In the summer of 1377 Catherine, accompanied by a group of her disciples, went to Rocca di Tentennano (also known as Rocca d'Orcia), which belonged to the Salimbeni family, to bring about peace between the two branches of that powerful Sienese clan now engaged in conflict, which civil and ecclesiastical authorities had tried in vain to bring to an end. First of all, Catherine suggested to the two principal victims of the stupid war — the sisters Bandera and Isa, now widowed by the deaths of their young husbands — that they retire from the world, become nuns of the religious community at Belcaro and love a Spouse who would never die. From the Rocca she made a pilgrimage, with her followers, to Montepulciano, where she won the poet Giacomo del Pecora to her point of view (he would later sing her praises) and then went on to Castiglioncello del Trinoro, where she induced the fierce Cione, leader of the opposing faction of the Salimbeni, to make peace. But she still had to deal with the inhabitants, particularly the scoundrels among them, many of whom had not received the sacraments for thirty or forty years — such hardened sinners that only Catherine could soften their hearts. This she did so well that the six or seven priests of the region were not enough to hear the confessions of those unfortunate people who, returning to God's friendship, returned also to a way of life less bestial. At one time they led Catherine to the balcony of the castle where there was a man possessed of the devil, screeching madly, bound hands and feet. Unafraid, serene, and solicitous, Catherine approached the creature, ordered him to be released from his bonds, then, putting her arm around his neck and drawing him down to her, she began to sob on his shaggy head. And with that gesture of love she cured him.

In the nearby abbey of St. Antimo, where she frequently went to pray in the great Romanesque church, crowds gathered about her and thousands of peasants returned to the Faith during the four months of her stay in that district. And along with the peasants were not a few notables of the region, among whom was the poet Anastasio da Montalcino. He has recorded in verse his impressions upon meeting "this Catherine . . . red rose, without thorns," writing among other things:

> From head down to her feet this humble maid
> With Christ is filled;
> Her glory on the day, the night
> In song is spilled.
>
> And as she looks to heaven her eyes
> Are wet with tears
> From which flow every good and grace
> Down through the years.
> . . . . . . . . . . . . . . . . . . . . . . . . . . . . . . . . . . . . . . . . . . .
> Standing before your altar here
> I see you, lovely Mother, venerable and dear.[2]

On the other hand, her stay aroused unjust suspicions of a political conspiracy, so that she was impelled to write to the heads of the Siena commune to remind them that both she and her followers were intent only upon the health of mind and body of the people. "I love you more than you love me," she reminds them, indicating delicately her surprise at their accusation.

She felt a stronger blow when she had to ask Fra Raimondo to leave Val d'Orcia and go to Rome to propose to the Pope certain plans for peace (possibly with Bernabò Visconti at the request of Acuto, now encamped with his mercenaries at San Quirico not far away) and word was brought back to her that the Pope had detained her spiritual father and son to make him prior at the Minerva.[3] It was an intimate and personal sorrow for Catherine to lose the soul that more than any other understood her, the priest who each day gave her Holy Communion and who better than any other understood her visions. It seemed that her last earthly consolation was gone and there remained nothing but shadows, ever growing more dense. Nevertheless she said to herself, "May the bitter will of God be done." Perhaps that separation, which caused both Catherine and Fra Raimondo to suffer, was due to the need which the Pope felt in having at hand as counselor a disciple of Catherine, since he had not been able to persuade Catherine herself to follow him to Rome, where he was now finding existence difficult.

For peace with Florence was further away than ever; the military ventures of the Pope's hired troops were ending in defeat; discontent and revolt shook almost the entire Peninsula, where only Queen Giovanna — an evil woman — seemed to remain faithful to him.

The net which the Florentine republic was weaving around the Pope continually attracted new allies, who promptly rebelled against the papal power, confining it more and more within a weak circle around Rome itself. Gregory XI lost all hope in the ambassadors of the Tuscan city but he still hoped in Catherine: disappointed in diplomacy and in armed might, he placed his hope in holiness; so he entrusted to Catherine, and to her alone, the task of making peace with Florence.

She obeyed. The wishes of the Pope were an order of Christ, and she resolved not to give up until the longed-for peace had been brought about.

At Easter time she sent a letter to the heads of the city; then in December (1377) she went in person, setting out from Rocca di Tentennano with a small company of her followers — the indispensable Alessia Cecca, Caterina di Ghetto, Neri, Stefano and, later on, Cristofano.

At Florence she was reverently received by Nicolò Soderini and other devout persons. It did not take long for her to grasp the mounting sacrilegiousness of the city, in contempt of the papal interdict. The churches all open in defiance of the papal decree indicated both the rebellious spirit of the populace and the cowardice of priests and laity who, to avoid trouble, had set themselves against the Church and their consciences. Manufacturing and business, weakened by the interdict, had lost their markets and their foreign credits. The populace was crushed and miserable; the crushing costs of the long war had occasioned the imposition of confiscatory taxes and various restrictions of ever increasing severity. In political life suspicion and private revenge were rampant under the guise of public welfare; the Eight of War did not want the conflict to end, for the reason that peace would have put an end to their regime. The leaders of the Guelph faction, under the pretext of rooting out Ghibellines, ruined the careers of men and threw them out of office upon the merest suspicion aroused by the calumnies of their personal enemies. As always happens, one of the results of the war was the twisting of consciences and the corruption of men's right sentiments, which provoked a gradual, but almost general, decadence of morals.

Amid that desolation Catherine set herself to proclaim peace and to strike out forcefully against all those who strove to continue a war that was ruining both the State and the Church, both the economic and the spiritual order.

The best citizens took Catherine's part; they could not but admire her disinterestedness, her burning charity, her sincere desire for peace. Because of her severity with herself, her charity and the good she accomplished, she was called by all "blessed." The trouble was, however, that the leaders of the Guelph party, under the pretext of going along with her, quite frequently made use of her name to justify acts of personal revenge, thereby arousing angry passions rather than promoting peace. They systematically set about condemning as "suspect" — that is, infected with Ghibellinism — not a few citizens who were perfectly innocent, always parading the name and authority of the young woman from Siena.

But Catherine held on, confiding in God alone. Gradually, almost imperceptibly, she sensed a ground swell for peace which, steadily growing, became a real political factor. This made her determined to call a top-level conference at Sarzana to settle the affairs of Italy. The meeting took place, with representatives of the Pope, the king of France, the queen of Naples, and the republics of Florence, Genoa, Venice, and Barnabò Visconti.

Meanwhile at Florence the new chief magistrate of justice, Silvestro dei Medici, hoping to diminish the abuses on the part of military leaders succeeded only in arousing the passions of the mob, already exasperated, ruined by the wars and economic crises produced by mercenary troops, epidemics and factional clashes. They decided upon an uprising to take place between June and August of 1378; and the insurrection culminated in the mob violence since called "dei Ciompi,"[4] which was nothing but a disordered uprising against the ruling classes, one of the disorders typical of the social crisis of contemporary Europe, torn asunder by petty wars, plagues, and ravaging troops of mercenaries, from which those most afflicted, the little people (called at Florence "the people of God") sought escape.

The savage hordes overwhelmed all police authority and attacked both good and bad, allowing themselves to be incited by the most irresponsible demagogues. The mob attacked and burned the home of the absent Soderini, whose only fault was that he was a follower of Catherine; they did the same to the house of Ristoro Canigiani, another disciple. Carried away by such fury, on June 22, a frantic mob went after Catherine herself, whom just a few days before they had called "blessed" and "saint." Yelling for blood, shouting imprecations, they assaulted her house.

Catherine, however, had been driven from the house by its cowardly owner, and she had gone with a few of her followers to pray in a garden nearby. Like Jesus in the garden, she was not surprised at the fickleness and ingratitude of men, for from infancy she had relied upon God alone. So in her prayer she asked the eternal Father to spare any more shedding of brothers' blood in this city entrusted to her striving for peace, but rather, if need there be for blood, to allow hers to be shed so that she might be united to Him.

While she prayed thus, the mob drew near, demanding Catherine of Siena, the hypocrite, the evil woman, that they might put her to death. Catherine arose and went to meet them. The first ruffian she encountered was brandishing a sword and shouting at the top of his voice: "Where is this Catherine?" Falling upon her knees before him, she said, "I am she. Kill me!" When the man hesitated Catherine said, "but I command in the name of God that you do no harm to any who are with me." She was at the mercy of the assassin, but she cared only for her companions.

Those words, which seemed more of heaven than of earth, showing the power of God in a pale, powerless girl, moved her would-be killer. Guilty, embarrassed, he could only mutter: "Go away . . . go away from me!" In vain she begged him not to disappoint her, now that the moment had come for her to offer this sacrifice for Christ and His Church. Followed by his gang, all breathless with expectation, the man with drawn sword, turned on his heel, and while Catherine's followers, still terrified and weeping, gave thanks to God, she herself showed her dismay, crushed with disappointment: "Miserable woman that I am — unworthy of martyrdom!"

Later on, writing to Fra Raimondo, she had to confess her regret at that martyrdom which failed — because, she said, of her own personal sins. Humiliated, she declared: "My Eternal Spouse has made a fool of me."

The episode had demonstrated, if further proof were necessary, the intrepidity of the Saint. She was all love; hence she knew no fear. And although, because of the popular obsession which was still at the boiling point, no one then or in the days to follow dared to offer her hospitality and all her friends urged her to flee from Florence and return to Siena, Catherine would not move; trusting in God, she hid wherever she could, first in a little room put at her disposition by a good man who venerated her and later on in a hermitage outside Florence. So little time remained for her; she had been sent by the Pope to bring about peace; and she must be about this business. Fortunately, when the first of demagogic madness had died down in Florence, the people saw her once more and listened to her as a creature from heaven. It was she herself who begged the Pope not to attach any importance to what had happened to her. And the poor Pope saw all his hopes vanish even as all around him resistance was crumbling. Florence was exhausted and in a state of decline by reason of her struggles against Church authority; but the temporal power of the Church, attacked by so many enemies, was falling apart, to the demoniac sneers of Bernabò, continually fomenting rivalries. Between revolts within the Church and rebellions from without, between palace conspiracies and clerical treason, the Pontiff sensed his helplessness and wished for the placid majesty of his Gothic manor on the banks of the Rhone. But he did not feel up to making a return trip.

So one night in March, after having devoutly received the last sacraments and having urged his cardinals to elect a worthy successor to him, Gregory XI died at the age of forty-nine, thinking, perhaps, of the one creature who had served him out of pure devotion.

The announcement of the Pope's premature death struck like lightning at a Christendom in which, amid an internecine war of Christians, there was being outlined in apocalyptic colors the clash between holiness and worldliness and men seemed asked to decide whether the Church should become once more a spiritual power such as Christ had established, depository of His sacred Blood and dispenser of the sacraments, or rather be completely transformed into a worldly power, now that dynasties gained more and more strength through a growing absolutism which could pour out blood in time of war and traffic in Church benefices in time of peace. In a babel of voices and theories the supreme episode of the conflict between religion and politics was at hand.

It is said that Gregory XI foresaw the conflict and, echoing Catherine's thought, attributed it to his own sins.

Thinking men everywhere realized that at the bier of the Pope Christendom stood at the brink of an abyss; everywhere men began returning to their native soil. So long as a Pope, no matter how vacillating, stood at the center of things, the clash could be, if not avoided, at least put off. But what would happen to his successor?

NOTES: *Chapter 27*
1. In Greek mythology, a crafty and avaricious King of Corinth, condemned in Hades to roll up a huge stone, which constantly rolled back.
2. English translation by Sister Madeleva, C.S.C.
3. The great Dominican convent of the Minerva, hard by the Church of Santa Maria sopra Minerva (built upon the ruins of a pagan temple) was the chief center of the Dominicans, as Ara Coeli was of the Franciscans. It was the residence of the Master General of the Dominicans.
4. Literally, "of the wooldressers."

# 28. The Schism

The election of Gregory XI's successor indicated the degree of the papacy's decadence. When the cardinals — sixteen in all — entered the conclave on April 7, 1378, a vast crowd of Romans — fearing the election of another Frenchman and the renewal of the Avignon episode — massed around the Vatican and cried over and over: "We want a Roman!" In that cry there was, above all, a revindication of the spiritual from the temporal, for by Roman they meant Catholic, papal, universal, and hence outside and above nationalism or dynasties; while French in that period of history meant infeudation to the court of France and, therefore, deformation of the Church into an organ of political government.

However, not everyone understood this; least of all those segments of the populace who, taking advantage of the general confusion, broke into the papal canteens and, becoming drunk, began to shout threats of death. The cardinals, terrified by the indecent shrieks coming up from the piazza about the possible election of Pedro de Luna,[1] elected the archbishop of Bari, Bartolomeo Preignano, who seemed to be a good compromise between Rome and Avignon since, although not a Roman neither was he a Frenchman; he was an Italian, a subject of Queen Giovanna and he enjoyed a good reputation.

Even then the cardinals feared that the mob, which continued to yell fierce threats, would not be satisfied; so they had an announcement made that a Roman had been elected, without giving his name; then in St. Peter's they put the pontifical robes on the aging Roman cardinal Tebaldeschi, who protested in vain against that comedy of fear, while the bells rang out festively and clergy and people broke out in a noisy *Te Deum.*

The next day the truth was out — that Cardinal Prignano had been elected; an official communique to this effect was issued to all Christendom with the assent of the entire sacred College. Now that they had overcome their fear, all the cardinals rendered the customary homage to the newly-elected Pope and asked him for the usual privileges. And on the 18th of the month, at the conclusion of a magnificent procession across the city, they celebrated his coronation at the Lateran, where the new pontiff was acclaimed under the name of Urban VI.

The new Pope was unusually gifted. He realized that unless the clergy were reformed everything would go to pieces. And he set to work immediately. But he went at it with more violence than prudence. He believed that there was question not so much of converting souls as of crushing resistence and he spoke to cardinals and princes and noblemen with a harshness of language that bordered upon actual abuse. Writing to Catherine about him, the prior of the Carthusian monastery of Gorgona, Don Serafini, described him as a terrible man who frightened those he dealt with by his acts and his words, one who trusted in God and feared no man.

The cardinals were no saints; accustomed to luxury and license, they did not resign themselves to unexpected restrictions and repressing asceticism. Fearing the worst, thirteen of them retired to Anagni in May, under the pretext of summer heat, and there they set about conspiring to the end that, in August, they jointly declared that they had elected the Archbishop of Bari under coercion and fear of the Roman populace and that, therefore, the papal election was null and void from the beginning. On August 27, for greater protection, the cardinals betook themselves to Fondi, as guests of Onorato Caetani, and there, at the importunities of the King of

France, they elected another pope, Robert of Geneva, who took the name of Clement VII. So there was now an antipope; or — as Stefano Maconi, in a violent outburst of passionate confusion, would have it — an antidevil or antidemon.

To such depths had the Christian spirit sunk in those prelates that they seemed not to realize that by the simple fact of breaking Christianity and the Church into two pieces they were completely in the wrong.

All the efforts of Clement VII, the pseudo-pope, a cunning man and an able diplomat, were spent in seeking followers in the various courts; so that all the money which should have been spent in equipping a crusade was used to help Christians kill one another.

Clement VII, the antipope, had begun the new scission of Christendom; now, as was logical, he took off for Avignon. Germany, Poland, England, Flanders, and Italy (with the exception of Naples) remained obedient to the true Pope, whose juridical position had been repeatedly proclaimed by all the cardinal electors up until May. The Queen of Naples, a corrupt and voluble woman, supported the antipope because she did not like the idea of a Pope who took his position seriously and because, holding her throne only through continuous intrigue, she preferred a pope in a faraway Avignon rather than in nearby Rome. France, Savoy, and Piedmont also gave allegiance to the antipope. Spain remained neutral.

Whatever may have been Pope Urban's faults, this schism in the Church was the direct result of the grave and complex crises which plagued the late Middle Ages. Particularly it was the fruit of bitter political strife. At Avignon the papacy had been caught up in the clash of ambitious and grasping rulers and it had become the worst victim of that struggle, for the cardinals developed into servitors of the courts of Paris and Madrid rather than of the court of Avignon and had allowed international politics to divide the Church. The reverse of the picture was that all political divisions had polarized, according to particular interests, in religious scission, so that each state could more plausibly plunder and kill in the name of the father of the faithful. The Middle Ages were crumbling; feudalism was breaking up; yet no new order appeared. In the confusion and lack of equilibrium social classes and interests were at war with one another, assuming the aspects of political movements and seeking always to exploit the forces of religion. So now, under the confusion resulting from two claimants to the papacy, opposing blocs in Christendom justified their fratricide. The net result, after so many years of simony, interdicts, excommunications, and scandals, was to drag public morality to appalling decadence, a decadence into which was inserted the rebirth of pagan literature, the repaganization of social ideas and practices, along with a growing absolutism which made people the personal property of kings. Gradually in the minds of the masses faith in things of heaven was transformed into reliance upon things of this earth; the liberty of the communes was at the mercy of royal caprice, all this with an intensity that, despite religious practices and rhetorical protests, became for many people the totality of life. The Redemption, which is liberty, was failing; tyranny was in the ascendancy.

It is not to be wondered at, then, if often even the saints did not understand what was going on and that they allowed themselves to be divided in a divided Christianity. If enlightened spirits like Catherine of Siena, Catherine of Sweden, Blessed Peter of Aragon, Blessed Orsolina of Parma, and Gerard de Groote, stood on the side of the legitimate Pope, on the other hand saints of the caliber of Vincent Ferrer, Colette, and Blessed Peter of Luxemburg were on the side of the illegitimate pope. Indeed in general, and for reasons understandable enough, among which the inadequacy of news reports in an age of difficult communications, the saints, just like the rest of the faithful, went along with their own governments and their own people. The same thing happened in religious communities, universities, and academies, and among prominent theologians.

There was actually a period in which Christendom had three popes — or rather, a pope and two antipopes. Only in 1417 did there come an end to the schism with the revolt of the people of Christendom, embittered and worn out by that intrigue of low politics, simony, and basest passions, in the web of which the dignity of Peter had been torn to shreds. On June 22, the threat made upon Catherine's life, in the bloody light of that atrocious wrangle, assumes the value of a symbol: as if it were an attempt to suppress, once for all, the Church in her person, in its virginal purity and love that knows no factions, and thus to remove the last barrier to the slaughter of civilization.

After the attempt upon her life, Catherine retired with a group of followers to a country retreat at Casentino, near Vallombrosa; whence she returned to Florence to take up again her efforts for peace, at the service of the Pontiff and the Florentines. She wrote her first letter to the new Pope, then residing at Tivoli, expressing the desire to see him securely established in true and perfect charity, so that as authentic supreme pastor of the Church, he might be ready to lay down his life for his flock: an offering that he would be prepared to make only if he were free from all self-love, and hence of fear. She admonished him not to separate mercy from justice, pointing out that, since the body of the Church was plagued by evils, it was all the more urgent that the head of the Church should conform himself to Christ crucified, of whose blood the Church was the dispenser, especially at a time so grave when prelates themselves instead of giving forth the good odor of virtue were actually, like evil-smelling growths, tainting the world with their "miserable and profligate vices": swindlers gambling with consecrated hands, simoniacal, avaricious, dissolute.

In another letter to Pope Urban she again admonished: "No more simony, no more unbridled luxuries, no more dealers in blood, no more swindlers in what ought to be the temple of God." Reform, then, to be effected energetically but at the same time with charity and justice, by choosing "a group of the holiest men, conspicuous for their virtues and not afraid to die. . . . And do not strive for grandeur. And appoint good cardinals . . . Oh, how happy my soul will be when I shall see rendered to the Spouse of Christ what is rightfully hers. . . ."

Then there was the matter of bringing about peace in Florence: she prayed and insisted, in the name of Christ crucified, that the Pope receive back into the fold the wandering sheep there.

"Alas, my father, that I should be still needed at Florence, for now it is time to bring this matter to a close. Do with me as you wish. . . . I cannot say more to you. Abide in the holy and sweet love of God. Most holy father, pardon my presumption; but my love and my grief must be my excuse to Your Holiness. Humbly I ask your blessing. . . ."

In this matter she hoped for the collaboration of Cardinal Pedro de Luna, upon whom she urged fortitude "as a pillar of strength in the garden of the Church, established in charity and wisdom and a good life": a life illumined by reason, in which the soul would be queen and sensuality the slave; thus to be a free son of God. Catherine feared — and with reason — that the Cardinal would vacillate under the pressures and persecutions of the clergy; hence she adjured him to rid himself of all self-love, the source of weakness.

"I have the impression that discord is arising there between Christ on earth and his disciples. This causes me intolerable grief, for the fear that I have of heresy which may come about as a punishment of my sins. Hence I beg you, in the name of that glorious and precious Blood . . . never to depart from virtue or from the side of the Pope."

Catherine sensed in the air an ecclesiastical rebellion and she was horrified at the thought of a division (she called it heresy) in comparison with which any war or any dishonor or any sort of catastrophe would have been, in her opinion, a "bit of straw or a mere shadow"; to avoid it she was prepared, God knows with what alacrity, to shed her blood.

Pope Urban VI, who at Avignon had known and admired Catherine, liked her suggestion for the pacification of Florence, knowing that no matter what happened she would be on the side of God and hence of the Holy See. So he sent to Florence an ambassador of peace, who, on the evening of July 18, entered the city on horseback, bearing aloft an olive branch, amid wild rejoicing of the people. Happy now, Catherine obtained a piece of the olive branch and distributed bits of it to her companions as a happy omen. After the return of the Pope to Rome, the pacification of Florence was Catherine's greatest political triumph.

She had labored for peace without counting dangers and fatigue, and now she had completed her task; so at long last, as she had desired, she could leave Florence and return home.

After leaving Florence, she wrote a letter to the city fathers, explaining that one of her motives for departing was her desire not to be the occasion of any disagreements among them, remembering that the devil had once sown in their hearts a series of suspicions regarding her activities. She sent them an augury of unity, the re-establishment of harmony among citizens. And she concluded: "I depart from you consoled because I have been able to accomplish what I proposed to do when I entered your city, and not to leave, even though it would cost me my life, until I should see you, his sons, reconciled with your father.... Yet I leave you in sorrow and with presentiment...."

Her presentiment was justified by the threats of revolt that rumbled under the cover of economic and social and spiritual distress. Other disorders were indeed imminent.

At any rate, with peace re-established between the Florentines and the Pope and with the interdict now abrogated, Catherine was on her way back to Siena, stopping on the way for a bit of fresh air and rest at the farm of her sister-in-law, Lisa, near San Rocca a Pilli. And indeed she has need of some rest; for the first reports of the plotting of the cardinals and hence of the threat of a schism began to lacerate her soul, for it seemed to this sensitive daughter of the Church that these disorders came about as a result of her sins and her lukewarmness in writing, in acting and in praying. Contemplating the breakup of the Christian order, she wailed: "This is a time for weeping!" And she wept bitterly.

NOTE:  Chapter 28

1. Pedro de Luna, a Spanish cardinal-deacon. He joined the French cardinals in the election of Antipope Clement VII.

## 29. The "Dialogue of the Divine Providence"

Filled with this bitterness against herself, one morning she dragged herself to the most distant church of the district and, wearied by her physical and moral sufferings, she threw herself before the door, feeling unworthy to enter the house of her Father in the presence of her Spouse. With such horror she sensed the impending calamity to the Church that she knew not where to turn and felt crushed by it, like a criminal, because of her fancied failure to fulfill the mission entrusted to her by God.

"Miserable that I am," she groaned, "the cause of every evil! . . . I have sinned, O Lord; have mercy upon me!"

Thus prostrate, Catherine experienced in the depths of her soul the agony of Jesus, abandoned upon the cross, and suddenly she felt overwhelmed by a flood of fire and blood. It was the life of God streaming through her. In a flash she felt strong, purified, and joyous, so that she rose to her feet, walked confidently into the Church and approached the altar where, all radiant with love, she assisted at Mass and received Holy Communion.

It would appear that Catherine and her companions frequently made the trip — three hours afoot — from San Rocco to Siena; and along the road, among the wooded hills and beside noisy brooks, they would stop to speak and sing the praises of God in whom, exchanging their love, they were all made one: they all became Catherine, as it were, in order to be all Jesus Christ.

Just outside the gates of Siena they would encounter hermits who lived in grottos or rude huts, and converse with them upon pleasant topics, thus escaping momentarily from a sorrowing world, that world which is the enemy of the Church, the world in which schism was already a black cloud loaded with storms.

And when disaster struck, with the election of an antipope on September 20, the voice of the Eternal became more insistent than ever; and in October, 1378, in a place of solitude that belonged to her follower, Fra Santi, who had been a companion of Colombini, Catherine dictated what is now known as the "Dialogue of Divine Providence," although the original title was simply *Book*.[1] During the dictation she was "abstracted," that is in mystical ecstasy, speaking all the while with the Father.

Reporting her words were her most faithful disciples: Barduccio, Stefano, Neri. The dictation lasted five whole days, from October 9 to 13, and was almost continuous, resulting in a book that was remarkable also for its size.

This book constitutes a sort of *summa* of Catherine's teachings, which she had previously imparted bit by bit, according to circumstances, in the fevered years of her apostolate. In it the saint reveals the mystical teaching which reviews the needs of the world; it rises to heaven and descends into hell, to serve the needs of earth; it asks the Father for light to enlighten her fellow men. The theology is sound, inspired; in it one realizes that the Holy Spirit, breathing where He will, now breathes into the mind of a semiliterate young woman, an intellectual power by which scholastic teaching is given a new direction and a fresh approach, so as to make the book something of the same order as the *Summa* of St. Thomas Aquinas, and to cause Pope Pius II, in his bull canonizing Catherine, to describe her teachings, as we have said, as inspired by the Holy Spirit.

It is symptomatic that in this book, as in many other expressions,

God appears to her above all as Truth, so that she speaks to the world as a teacher of Christian truth.

The name *Dialogue* has been given to the book, because it is substantially an exchange of questions and answers between the virgin daughter and the Eternal Father: this singular ascent to the Father, while it marks the height that may be reached by the soul also shows the universal character of the longed-for reform in the world, with its treatises on the divine fatherhood, signifying power and mercy, justice and charity. The world, wounded in its sense of brotherly love, on the verge of a terrible fracture in the Mystical Body of Christ, the first-born Brother, needed a new statement of the Fatherhood of God, in which all men could feel themselves united as brothers; a statement that must be, after all, a repetition of the Gospel, an expression of the love of the Father through the mouth of His Son.

Theologically the book, characterized by Catherine's simple, feminine personality, suggests the intellectual depth of Thomas Aquinas; furthermore it bears the mark of Dominican realism, through which union with God becomes a passion of love for men, just as Aquinas' reasoned exposition of dogma was the fruit of the adoring love of a poet. In the Dominican tradition Catherine also thus understood the maxim: *contemplari et contemplata aliis tradere.*[2]

The book was so well received by Catherine's followers that they made it their daily spiritual food; and they copied it and translated it into Latin for circulation throughout the world.

In a letter to Fra Raimondo who, in the book as in the heart of the authoress, occupies a place of first order, she herself gives a sort of summary of the work. The *Dialogue* was born of four petitions which Catherine, in ecstasy, addresses to the Father, to implore His mercy: (1) for herself; (2) for the world; (3) for the Church; (4) for a particular case. But around these points Catherine develops and weaves in subjects of general interest, especially in that epoch plagued by error and war.

Catherine's teachings are clarified with a more sorrowful insistence upon their social implications, associating more vitally, so as to make them practically identical, the love of God and the love of neighbor. He who loves God "does usefully" for his neighbor: this is the criterion of the Christian's conduct. "Love of Me and of neighbor is one and the same thing," our Lord tells Catherine; "and just to the extent that the soul loves Me it loves him, because love for him comes from Me." One's neighbor is the *means* — almost the mediator — by which man, not being able to help God, who has no need of his help, helps his brothers, and makes this service universal. In this *means* — in one's brother — virtues and vices are tested. In a more particular manner, however, it is the condition of the poor that becomes associated with that of Christ, and in the defense of the poor are castigated, as by swords of fire, every sort of profanation and abuse: avarice, usury, plundering, and rapine.

In the light of this dialectic Catherine evaluates the process of becoming bold, so necessary to all. In this process she comes to define the value of penance, subordinated to that of virtue; the one a means of augmenting the other, and to be employed with discretion and humility, and never to be esteemed for itself alone. The basis of a life of perfection is love. "Hence perfection does not consist solely in macerating the flesh but in conquering one's own perverse will. And in this way of the will, denying itself and subjecting itself to My will, you should desire, and I want you to desire, that all may go." All: this is Catherine's universal message: to substitute for one's own will, the seat of evil, the will of God, fount of all good. This substitution is the most powerful act of free will. "This is the teaching of light."

Love, translated into service of our brethren, unites us with them and unifies us with God: and thus it divinizes us by means of our brothers. In prayer Catherine exclaims: "We are Thy image and Thou art our image. . . . Why? Because of love. Thou, God, are made man and man is made God. For this cause, ineffable Love, I implore Thee to show mercy to Thy creatures."

Thus the vision of the book is rounded out: it begins with sin, with hell, and culminates in the enjoyment of God: the fate of the soul that seeing, recognizes, and recognizing, loves ("love comes after the intellect and the more one knows the more he loves") and loving, tastes of God, the Supreme Good, and tasting God, denies its own will, to make it God's will: and God's will is our sanctification on earth that will merit us the beatific vision in heaven. When our own will becomes the will of God, the soul bears with reverence and perseverance every trial sent by Him, or permitted by Him, accepting it and using it as a means of grace: it comports itself as Jesus upon the cross, blessed and suffering; suffering in body, blessed in soul. United in her will with God she is made one with Him and He one with her. The passage from the human to the divine is made across a bridge, which is Jesus Christ Himself: a bridge thrown across a river which, flowing through the valley, continually assumes new forms, a figure of the changeable and transitory nature of all earthly things. Upon the bridge there is dispensed the blood of Christ, food for wayfarers and pilgrims: this is the Church, governed by the Vicar of Christ and his ministers.

The Church is Catherine's love and passion. The consciousness of the Church becomes, if possible, even more alive in the loving soul; and not only of the Church upon earth, of which for many years she has been the sentinel and herald and, in a certain sense, the vigorous, fighting leader, but the entire Church, from heaven to purgatory, for which she has been afflicted, offering her sufferings to complete those of the Redeemer and thus making satisfaction, on her own part, to divine justice: a daily collaboration with God through the Church.

In this identification of her soul with the spirit of the Church, Catherine has ever before her (and now she reaffirms it) the value of universality, for which she suffers and prays and feels herself in debt to everyone and to all; another Christ, nailed to the cross between earth and heaven, between men and God, she prays: "To Thee I fly, Eternal Father, in Thee I take refuge; and I pray not for myself alone but for all the world, and especially for Christ's Mystical Body, the Church; that this truth, this doctrine, shine forth in her ministers, since it has been given by Thee, eternal Truth, through Thy miserable servant. And I ask it especially for those whom Thou has given me and whom I love with a special love, who are one

with me; that they shall be my delight for the glory and praise of
Thy holy name." The Lord God taught Catherine: "Only he fears
who feels alone, who hopes in himself, deprived of love; he is afraid
of every little thing because he is alone, deprived of Me Who alone
can give security to the soul who possesses Me in the affection
of love."

He is not alone who is united to God and, through Him, is united
to his brethren, whom he serves as their subject even though he be
their superior, a servant even through the master, infirm even though
in good health, weak though powerful. He is not alone who, bound
to his brethren by the grace of the sacraments, makes up with them
the Mystical Body which is Christ.

If the real origin of evil is self-love, its principal external instrument is the abuse of riches, avarice for gain, and desire for pleasure.
And Catherine wishes to make both clergy and laity free from the
obsession of Mammon, under whose baleful influence quarrels break
forth, sins are committed and men lie terrorized in the servile fear
which makes slaves. He who hopes in God is not afraid; "but those
who hope in themselves . . . fear and are afraid of their own shadows,
and doubt that there is any real aid for them either in heaven or
upon earth. . . . Every evil, harm, and suffering in this life or in
the next comes from the love of riches. On the contrary . . . every
good, peace, repose and tranquillity comes from poverty."

In this sort of discussion, with these ideals, teachings, and exhortations, Catherine unmercifully unmasked the crude and unend-
ing reality of the struggle between God and Mammon; and her
apostolate, going to the very center of historical disturbances, tended
substantially to bring worshipers of Mammon back to God. In the
clergy, above all, the thirst for riches opened up abysses of vice.
Catherine gives us a realistic picture of the widespread corruption
of vice in ecclesiastical circles, the most relentless picture that we
have, all the more terrifying in that it comes from a virginal soul,
from angelic purity. She shows us the priests with their concubines,
surrounded by their children in churches and rectories and canonries,
in the streets and in the taverns; and she stigmatizes sins against

nature which, like leprosy, contaminate priests and laymen, rich and poor, unmindful of their miserable state, a stench so revolting that it is distasteful to the devils themselves; and she sees in these and other sins of impurity and of usury an effective barrier against the knowledge of God. Degraded into swindlers, robbers, effeminate creatures, servitors of their relatives, shameful lovers and usurers, these ministers of God, perverted and perverters of others, who have transformed the house of God into a den of thieves, go about as dead men burying the dead — they who should be living bearers of life. Caring for nothing but ostentation, ceremonial and riches, they speak a language "very clean," they who are filthy in mind and corrupted in thought. They are prone to such hypocrisy by the requirements of their state in life, which demands "an attractive personality," elegant and luxurious dress, "persons who should be devoted" and who should present an attractive soul in humility of life and sentiment. Thus it comes about that in naming prelates preference goes to the proud, to the smooth spoken, to those apparently cultured, to braggadocios. "They make much of knowledge, of science. Science in itself is a good and perfect thing, when the scientist has both knowledge and a good and honest life, with true humility." Otherwise, knowledge, with pride and immorality, becomes a poison: for in pride and in sin the light makes shadows. Hence, in the house of God, in which "the light of science should shine upon an honest and saintly life," only lies abound.

The formation of holy souls in the service of the Church is — also in this book — at the very center of Catherine's preoccupations and prayers. Trading in the sacraments and in ecclesiastical dignities is simply not to be tolerated. The faithful must support their priests by the contributions, but the priests themselves must divide their income into three parts: one for themselves, one for the poor, and one for the Church. "No other way is allowed." It is not permitted to amass wealth and then to leave an estate at death; it is advisable rather to leave the Church in debt if this be done to succor the poor. Worthy priests never need be afraid that they will lack anything, either temporal or spiritual.

Dispensers of the Blood of Christ, they must be dependent solely upon the Church, the treasury of this Blood — that is, upon the Pope, and not upon temporal lords. If priests are unworthy, however, it is not the business of the laity, neither is it the business of the civil law, to interfere; and their unworthiness does not take away the efficacy of the sacraments, which have their value exclusively from that Blood. Hence irreverence on the part of laymen toward priests can never be justified. For that matter, Catherine recalls both to priests and to laymen their obligations of justice and probity. "In no state of life can one obey the civil law and the divine law in a state of grace without holy justice." Justice is the very axis of the whole system — ecclesiastic and civil — which Catherine so longs for.

For everybody, but in a special way for religious and clergy, she holds obedience in highest esteem, not only for its intrinsic value but also for its disciplinary efficacy in an era of insubordination within the Church. Disobedience to the Vicar of Christ, to whom all owe homage unto death, is a factor in the desuetude of love, from which obedience, as any other virtue, takes its value. Among the obligations assumed with the gift of Faith, the Christian has first of all that of obeying the commandments of the law, beginning with that of love. The new man is the man who obeys; the old man is the man who disobeys. He who obeys, saves his soul; he who disobeys, loses it. "Oh, how sweet and glorious is this virtue, in which all other virtues are contained! It is conceived and brought forth in charity; it is the corner stone of our holy faith. . . ."

Obedience is associated with patience and produces joy.

Really obedient souls are they who "are not content with the commandments in general" but also follow the evangelical counsels, "actually and mentally," and through these bind themselves to a "particular obedience." "These wish to destroy in themselves all self-love and all their own will, to bind themselves more closely to God." And they bind themselves either by the vow of obedience in a religious order, or, outside a religious order, by submitting their will to that of some person. Both the former and the latter choose "most perfect obedience."

In writing thus Catherine was thinking of her followers; some of them subject to religious superiors; all of them bound by a "particular obedience" to her; and she sees in this arrangement a benefit for the individual souls and for all the Church.

On religious orders the measure of obedience is the measure of the spiritual life of its members and hence of the vitality of each order. Each religious order, infallibly approved by the Holy See, has in itself the necessary means for the sanctification of its members; however, through the unfaithfulness of its subjects, and primarily through disobedience, it may be deformed and thus deviate from the right path. Every founder impresses upon his community a characteristic, a particular virtue, although all orders are founded in love, from which each one draws its life. Thus to St. Francis belonged in a special manner the virtue of poverty; to St. Dominic, the virtue of knowledge; but if the Franciscan does not obey the commandment of poverty and the Dominican the duty of wisdom, he degenerates. Obedient, for example, was St. Thomas Aquinas who, "with the gentle eye of his intellect" speculated upon divine truth, "where he acquired supernatural light and infused knowledge through grace. . . . Truly Dominic and Francis were two pillars of Holy Church: Francis with his poverty . . . Dominic with his wisdom."

NOTES: Chapter 29

1. The Dialogo della Divina Providenza is a volume of 503 pages in the Italian text edited by Fr. Taurisano. It contains 167 short chapters. St. Catherine called her work the *Book*; her followers called it the *Dialogue*. The reason for the title *Dialogue* stems from the fact that the saint in the first 13 chapters tells of making four requests of our Lord; the remainder of the book contains the responses of our Lord to her, in the form of a doctrinal exposition.
2. "To contemplate and then pass on to others the fruits of our contemplation."

## 30. *Obedience*

The perfectly obedient, in the ranks of a religious order, first of all liberate themselves from earthly riches and their own will, acquiring eternal riches of humility, of patience, of continence, of justice, of prayer, of vigilance, of labor — all in the light of faith.

But also outside of a religious order, Christians may well observe the perfection of the evangelical counsels, Catherine writes, "some in the virginal state, others in chastity, though no longer virgins. They observe obedience . . . submitting themselves to a superior, whom they endeavor to obey with perfect obedience until death. And if you were to ask me which is more meritorious, those who are in a religious order or those who are outside I should reply that the merit of obedience is not measured by the act or by the place, that is to say . . . more in the secular state than the religious, but according to the measure of love which the obedient one has . . . this is the real measure."

Thus in the *Dialogue* Catherine sums up her experiences and at the same time brings into harmony the attitudes she has taken. She is the pulsating, burning heart of a system which embraces all creatures in God; her bold and farseeing mind contemplates in Him all the aspects of life. She presents herself now as a teacher of theology and philosophy, now as a writer and psychologist, but above all as a director of souls and a guide of Christian peoples. She knows the standard for transforming those masses into an organic Church and of remaking of Christianity the pure Mystical Body of Christ. She is not the detached observer, gazing out over a boundless horizon; rather, she is the watchman who goes about like a living flame in a dark night, or the teacher who at each step rediscovers the divine aspect of things, with a real feeling for life and a faith in substantial values, dissipating shadows and checking evil: an angel of light, poised in Christendom against the darkness of Babylon.

The *Dialogue* is in a word a *vade mecum* of the pure morality of the Gospel which needed to be restated and inculcated in an hour of perversion. And since she felt those truths so strongly and used them at times like whips, at night, after dictating such pages of fire, she suffered keenly to compensate divine justice in the name of the sinners she had castigated and to stimulate, by prayer and bloody sweat, the recognition of the values of the Redemption, obliterated by the voluntary slavery of men, who, created by God without their willing it, would not be saved by Him without their willing it. We can see now that in the hour of darkness the Holy Spirit raised up in Catherine a striking manifestation of Holy Church; that in a certain sense He made of her the expression and the symbol of the true Church which is nourished, and in turn nourishes souls, with the incorruptible Blood of the Lamb.

Catherine is the advocate of holiness, the guardian of truth. She is the herald of the true servants of God and the protectress of the humble, the poor, the victims of that vast, unclean wickedness, the product of the degradation of religion, both within and without the Curia, of the monasteries, of canonries, of families. It would seem that the mercy of God in heaven and the revolt of Catherine on earth combined to keep Christendom from being devoured by the jaws of the Evil One. It would seem that she, a real copy of Christ and fused in Him, was interposed between creatures and the Creator to re-establish the communion, interrupted and often broken off, by the traumata of sin.

In a period of bewilderment she gives anew a direction and a significance to existence: the direction of the divine and the significance of an ascent to God. She gives strength again to a people oppressed by fear, recalling all men to the beauty of sanctity, in which the soul, though existing in a mortal body, may even now taste immortality and, receiving everything from the hand of God, accepts tribulation along with consolation, life along with death; without being discouraged, always unafraid, founded upon a living rock.

This young woman of Siena thus stands as an apostle and a prophet; as a judge and a censor; she shouts above the roof tops and in the midst of the tempest; and she ignites a fire; faithful, tenacious, powerful interpreter of the will of that God whom she, from the depths of her nothingness invokes: "O eternal Father! O fire and abyss of Love! O eternal Beauty, O eternal Wisdom, O eternal Goodness, O eternal Mercy, O eternal Hope, O Refuge of sinners, O ineffable Bounty, O eternal and infinite Good, O violent Love! Hast Thou really need of Thy creature? . . . Strange as it seems. . . ."

# 31. At Rome

In the *Dialogue*, therefore, we contemplate, in the divine sphere, the drama of the soul and of the Church in a critical hour of her history; something of the rapture of an apocalypse, reaching up to heaven for enlightenment and energy, and then taking up again on earth, with more force than ever, the perennial fight against the error of antichrist and his seizure of souls, to bring them back to the reality of the Redemption.

Back down to earth, fortified by the vision of heaven, Catherine returns to the lists, like a standard bearer of the Church militant. With her disciples gathered about her Catherine longs to go to Rome to defend Urban VI; she now writes letters of fire — the boldest and most vehement of her audacious career — and she places herself completely at the disposition of the Pope, whose legitimate juridical position she proclaims loudly, with all the vigor of logic. In this action of hers, holiness and realism (one might say, heaven and earth) are fused in a Catholic politics which defends the rights of God and of man, of the Church and of the State, with clear and marvelous intuition. In that dark night of Christendom she blazes like a burning torch. In the midst of timidity, base calculations, ambitions, and dissensions, her virginal uprightness and honesty shine like a lily in the midst of a miry bog. Like Mary, she alone is like an army set in battle array.

It is she who gives the Pope courage, who reminds him of the dignity and authority of his office and exhorts him to take up again the tradition of irreproach which had always characterized the Vicars of Christ, surrounding himself with counselors and functionaries of unstained lives, now that he was freed of traffickers in blood. Only Catherine would dare to advance this sort of advice, to make such suggestions to a Pope, and a Pope easily angered, a Pope who had dealt harshly with one of her messengers (Fra Bartolomeo Dominici). However everyone understood from what faith and from what humility such counsel came. Catherine lived for the Church, for the Papacy; she was prepared to die for them; the torture of the Vicar of Christ was her martyrdom. In the midst of the disorders afflicting men's souls she had invited the Pontiff in all charity and patience to conform himself to the stricken Christ, reviled, killed, while she deplored the fact that "demons incarnate" had elected an antichrist against Christ upon earth. In this conflict, Catherine declared, one could see who was a lover of himself and who was a lover of truth: as for herself, she was eager to place her life and the lives of her followers in jeopardy to give testimony to the true head of the Church before the world.

Pope Urban, living in Latium,[1] was the target of all sorts of threats from kings and other powerful rulers; but he did have on his side a pure and invincible power: Catherine of Siena.

When she learned of the election of the antipope, Catherine was seized by a great righteous anger; she immediately wrote to the three Italian cardinals, Orsini, Corsini, and Brossano, casting into their teeth their contradictions in first presenting Urban VI as the legitimate Pope and then repudiating him as illegitimate. After refuting their sophisms, she calls them stupid, blind, liars, and idolaters, and the more guilty in that ("humanly speaking") they are Italians and yet do not feel for an Italian Pope that "passion for their native land" that motivated the others, especially the French. She wrote also to the Queen of Naples; and to the Count of Fondi, protector of the false pope, upbraiding him with "doing the work of the devil," exhorting him and adjuring him, in charity and truth, speaking "securely but irreverently" as she had written to the queen, her "dearest mother" if "obedient to Holy Church" but "a servant and slave of the devil," and hence to be mourned "as if dead" if she persisted in her disobedience.

The Pope well understood the importance of Catherine's assistance; and desiring to have her near him, he commanded her to come to Rome. This was just what Catherine wanted. Yet now, at the moment of resolving to leave Siena, she hesitated, not for herself but for the others, in view of the gossip already being circulated among old women of both sexes, certain to be amplified and to become bitterer upon her departure. According to these scandalmongers, a nun who went traipsing around the country with a company of followers, among whom, besides, were young men like Stefano Maconi always attached to her skirts, spending money all over the place, was a discredit to her home and her country, to her religious order and to the Church. In much the same way Jesus had scandalized the inhabitants of Nazareth by not attending to the carpenter's shop and wandering around Palestine to proclaim ideas good for nothing but to arouse disorders. "Good" people, petrified in the inertia of the spirit and in the unchangeableness of history, would not tolerate innovations, especially by persons whom they knew, born of the poorer classes, who would do well to mind their own business. An apostolate that rises above the ordinary is seen by them as fanaticism or a mania for human glory. Tradition is seen by them not as a tree that grows but as a trunk that rots.

So Catherine, unburdening herself in a letter to Fra Raimondo, asks him, in case the Pope really wants her to come that the Pontiff should send her a written order, so as to close the mouths of her maligners.

The written order came forthwith; and Catherine left Siena in the middle of November, followed by Barduccio, ever more devoted and trustworthy, by Neri and Gabriele Piccolomini, Fra Bartolomeo, maestro Tantucci, Fra Santi, and four of her nuns. She arrived in Rome on November 28, to be greeted by the faithful Fra Raimondo who was in touch with the Pope. A little later it would seem, her mother, Lapa, called "grandma" by Catherine's followers, arrived in Rome. The Pope was comforted by the coming of this daughter of his, worth more to him than all his other supporters put together, and he accorded her a solemn audience, surrounded by the cardinals whom he had named. The ambassador of Siena, Lando Ungaro, writing from Rome on November 30 to the heads of Siena about this audience said: "Catherine of Monna Lapa has come here and Our Lord the Pope has gladly received her and listened to her. What he asked her is not known; but it is apparent that he is happy to have her here." Catherine expressed herself forcefully to those assembled and she convinced that important gathering by the charm and logic of her luminous faith. The Pontiff himself gave expression to the collective sentiment of admiration, almost of dismay, which Catherine aroused, when he declared: "This little woman confounds us. For while we are afraid, she stands without fear, and by her persuasions she gives us courage."

Indeed her intrepidity inspired virility, so that the Pope could add: "What should the Vicar of Christ fear, even though the whole world be ranged against him? The omnipotent Christ is more powerful than all the world, and it is inconceivable that He would abandon His holy Church."

Pope Urban then asked her to go to the court of Queen Giovanna of Naples to persuade her to reconsider her attitude; and he suggested as her companion the daughter of St. Bridget, another Catherine, also a saint, Karin of Vadstena. It is surprising, certainly, to see the Pope, and in his person, the Church militant, place himself in the chaste hands of two women, one thirty-two years old, the other, forty-six, as the most vigorous and intelligent protagonists that could be found.

The Swedish woman was in Rome for the purpose of advancing the canonization of her mother. Surprised by the schism, she energetically took the side of Pope Urban. However, when it was proposed that she betake herself to Naples she declined the mission, having no confidence in the perfidious queen, of whose lascivious life she had had an unpleasant experience upon her return voyage from the Holy Land in company with her mother. Fra Raimondo, sharing the Swedish woman's conviction, convinced the Pope not to send the two women to Naples. The intervention of the friar, however, aroused Catherine's indignation: it seemed to her an indication of timidity, unworthy of the traditions of a Catherine of Alexandria, a Margaret, an Agnes, or other sainted virgins. The idea seemed to her not to be motivated by prudence but rather by a lack of faith.

This was the new fact, astounding in the midst of a Christendom shot through with violence but completely lacking in fortitude: this young Sienese woman was never afraid. Popes, cardinals, kings, military leaders experienced fear and therefore resorted to conspiracies. Catherine worked in the light of the sun, she said what she thought, she moved without hesitation; she loved and therefore she was not afraid. With love — she had dictated in ecstasy for her *Dialogue* — one may become another Christ, one may share in His omnipotence.

Meanwhile, transported by an interior fire, Catherine lost no time in idleness. Her residence at the foot of the Pincio[2] was a retreat of the Sienese in Rome; people flocked there to seek her aid in gaining audiences, privileges, various indulgences from the Vatican or from Santa Maria in Trastevere, where the Pope had taken refuge to be safer from the fortress of Castel Sant' Angelo,[3] now in the hands of the French faction of Limoges.

"The indulgences which you ask," she wrote to Maconi, "I shall make it a point to beg from the Pope along with the first I ask of him; I cannot say just when this will be, however, for I am getting to be a nuisance with the notaries of the Curia." She housed as many persons as she could, to the point where at times, together with her twenty-four followers, there were from forty to sixty in all, devoted persons for whom, not having anything of her own, she had to beg food — which was never wasted, nor yet ever lacking.

One day when they were almost without bread she was able completely to satisfy the hunger of all by serving them what she had on hand. An active and practical woman, while she was contemplatively absorbed in God she entrusted the direction of the house in turn each week to one of her companions, who was required to render an account each evening of her administration; Catherine supervised everything like a prudent housewife.

It had probably been Fra Raimondo who had found that house for her. He had always remained affectionately bound to her. Furthermore his wisdom and grasp of doctrine had made him dear also to the Pope, so that he was chosen to lead a papal mission to the King of France, Charles V, in an endeavor to bring him back to allegiance to the true Pope. It was a difficult mission; the journey would be dangerous and Fra Raimondo would have to be separated from Catherine. She also would feel the separation but she enthusiastically encouraged him to do as the Pope wished in all confidence. For her, Fra Raimondo agreed to go. In their parting conversation Catherine urged him: "Now go, with God; I think that we shall not again in this life be able to speak at length as we have now spoken."

Catherine accompanied Fra Raimondo to his embarkation; and as the boat shoved off she knelt on the bank and, after having prayed a while, she traced the sign of the cross in the direction of the vessel as if clearly to say: "You, my son, will be safe, for the sign of the cross will protect you, but in this life you will not again see your mother." Then she wept.

Separated from Catherine, Fra Raimondo, although a man of faith, lost his courage; and at Ventimiglia, having learned that the schismatics were concocting a brutal attack upon the papal legation, he called off the trip and, with the permission of the Pope, returned to Genoa with the intention of influencing various adversaries scattered along the Riviera. Catherine was not happy about the retreat: humanly speaking it was understandable, but in the divine plan it meant weakness. She wrote to Fra Raimondo: "You were not worthy to stand on the field of battle; like a boy you became frightened and then fled. My perverse father, how blessed would my soul have been had you been brave enough to have sealed with your blood another stone in the fortress of Holy Church. . . ."

The Pope now entrusted to her a Bull inviting the most reliable persons she knew to come to Rome and place themselves at his disposal. She seized the opportunity to bring to Rome a coterie of holiness, souls most securely dedicated to God. "Do not delay, for the love of God; do not delay. . . . Come, come and not wait for time because time will not wait for you." Thus she wrote impatiently to the prior of Gorgona, to the hermits of Lecceto, and to others. However, these appeals were not well received by certain older individuals — to whom they seemed to lack prudence. The reply of the learned English hermit of Lecceto, Fra William Fleet, for example, was a painful disappointment; her urgent prayers for him to hasten to Rome to lend a hand with the crusade against the schism brought the terse response that his duty was to attend to his prayers in his silent woods rather than look for action in a decadent city. To Catherine's way of thinking this repulse meant that the hermit was unwilling to lose himself for the honor of God, unwilling to understand that the time had come to go out into the streets, to shout from the housetops and to do battle in the fields. She replied with irony: "It would seem that God is to be found only in the woods and nowhere else — even in a time of dire necessity!" The meek English hermit, Fra James, sent from Selva del Lago one of his confreres, Fra Antonio; he himself, in his hermitage, set about gathering documents in support of the cause of Pope Urban, which were to exercise a powerful influence upon his far-off fellow citizens in England.

At Rome, Catherine, unresigned to the timorousness of those who had impeded her trip to Naples, besides sending Neri to that city, continued to write to the queen and to various women of influence in that kingdom to bring them over to the cause of the Pope. She had plunged into the midst of the fray and she fought as in a crusade, encouraging her followers to give their lives for the holy cause, lamenting that she could not better her words by putting them into action. She realized that in that frightening crisis the longed-for reform was in jeopardy, there being question now either of abandoning the Church into the predatory hands of royal politics or of vindicating the dignity of the Mystical Body. Hence, she could not understand all the delays and reservations. She would have liked to mingle her blood with the Blood of Christ, but in vain she prayed: "My Love, my Love, grant me to die." To her love, made up of fire and blood, that existence woven of compromise be-

tween God and the world, between pope and antipope, between virtue and vice, in which most men were bogged down, seemed like
a living death; avid for the absolute, she longed to be immersed in
love eternal. To Stefano, who had remained at Siena, she wrote
urgently: "Flee from the world; leave your home."

Christmas came, and as a loving and ingenuous daughter she sent
a gift to the pope, "the sweet Christ upon earth" — five oranges
she had gilded, and a letter. Then came the carnival of 1379 which
recalled her espousal to Jesus, celebrated twelve years before, in far-
off Siena, where even now so many of her disciples awaited her; she
loved them all with a singular love, and thought of them one by
one. Then Lent, during which she, no doubt, joined the Romans in
procession to the various stational churches. At the end of April
the troops of the antipope, some holed up in Castel Sant'Angelo and
others deployed along the Alban hills, were defeated by Alberico
da Balbiano both at Rome and at Marino. The Pope — to Catherine's
admiration — took part, barefooted, in a procession of thanksgiving
from Santa Maria in Trastevere to San Pietro. To hasten the final
victory of Urban, Catherine sent to Alberico, to the Queen of Naples,
to Charles V, and to the seven military leaders of Rome, four famous
letters, dictated simultaneously in ecstasy, in which political action
was exalted to a supernatural plane, made once more an instrument
to attain that supreme end of the life of each man and of all: God
Himself. Hers seems to be a desperate undertaking against enormous
odds, against age-old habits of inertia, fear, and vice.

She had in mind the Kingdom of God: that system in which, with
the suppression of personal ambitions, men would live only to do
the will of their Father; and she seemed alone against all the rest.
Perhaps at her suggestion, the Pope again asked Fra Raimondo to
leave Genoa and to go, by way of Catalaunia, to France, there to
win over to Urban's side Emperor Charles V, whose allegiance to the
antipope was not as unwavering as it seemed, for he looked to a
general council for a solution. But again this time Fra Raimondo
parried the request, not trusting Cardinal Pedro de Luna, who had
caused the King of Aragon to arrest the emissaries of Urban VI in
Spain. Once more Catherine was embittered. She had worked so

hard to mold the pure soul and open mind of that Dominican friar into a man of fortitude, and now, at the test, he had failed her again and become flabby with the diplomatic prudence of a servant who was a good man but certainly no hero. In reproving her absent disciple she also accused herself of a lack of love and hence of faith in her Lord, unworthy, therefore, of the tradition of the martyrs. And blaming herself for Fra Raimondo's weakness, she found the cause, as usual, to be the self-love not yet rooted out of her soul.

Fra Raimondo began to fear that their relationship would deteriorate, that the bond of particular love between them would be broken. But Catherine assured him that such thoughts, aroused by the devil, had no foundation. "But if you had been faithful," she wrote to him, "you would not have been so vascillating, would not have lost confidence in God and in me, but as an obedient son you would have gone forward and done what you could. And if you could not have marched upright you could have crawled on all fours; if you could not have gone as a friar, you could have gone as a pilgrim; and if you had no money, you could always beg. Such faithful obedience would have wrought more in the sight of God and in the hearts of men than all possible human prudence."

An obedience of one who is dead to himself, that is, service to the Church and to the Pope of one who is dead to himself, hence oblivious to persecutions and sufferings — such is Catherine's demand. By himself one can do nothing; in Christ he can do everything.

Such obedience is, of course, mystical. But it can be incarnate in everyday life. For her, God alone mattered. To live meant to lose herself in Him. By the grace of God she effected this continuing transformation by copying Christ crucified, that is, by accepting trials and sufferings and making them the food of growth. Everything for Him; and for His love, everything for her brethren; for herself, she did not exist. He who does not lose his life will not find it. One must always be a victim on the cross to continue the work of the Crucified. "We are the victims offered in the garden of Holy Church, to the Christ on earth, the master of this garden. Therefore, let us act like the dead. They neither see, nor hear, nor feel. . . I tell you, holy father, that whether we wish it or not, the times in which we live invite us to die. Wherefore I do not wish to see you any longer alive. . . . As you have been a man in promising . . . do not be a woman when we come to the driving of the nails."

Meanwhile at Naples, on May 13, the antipope, housed by the queen in the Castel dell'Ovo, on the gulf, was driven out by the fury of the Neapolitans and forced to flee; he escaped to Avignon where he took up residence on June 20. Rome and Avignon — even in topography the lines were drawn.

In vain Catherine wrote again to the queen of Naples, who, two years later, was to be suffocated with a pillow in her bedroom. Writing about her to King Louis of Hungary Catherine asked: "Will you permit that antichrist, a member of the devil, and a woman, plunge into darkness and ruin all our holy Faith?"

And she turned again to the rulers of Siena (among whom was a disciple of hers, Andrea di Vanni, a painter who was to leave us her best portrait on the walls of the chapel called "delle Volte"), as well as those of Perugia and of Florence, to urge them to fidelity and to the aid of the true Pope.

In autumn she learned that her Stefano, kept away from her, to his great sorrow, by the jealousy of his relatives, had fallen into the hands of the mercenaries of Acuto and had been liberated simply by invoking Catherine's name — a name still rich in prestige with that terrible marauder.

She became more active than ever, for she had prayed the Lord for action; and her action was the product of her faith. So in the face of failures due to weakness and betrayals she entered more and more into God. She felt consumed in Him. She had been writing continuously. At length, however, she turned to admonish herself: "Now keep silence, my soul, and speak no more." Instead of speaking now, she prayed harder, and spent time in contemplation. So passed the winter. Near the beginning of 1380, at the invitation of Cardinal Niccolo Caracciolo, a friend of hers as he had been of St. Bridget, she prayed in a particular way for the end of the schism, and offered her body as an anvil upon which the sins of the adversaries of the Pope might be hammered out. Night after night, desolated by the spectacle of the ingratitude of the Roman people toward their bishop, Pope Urban, she repeated the offering. More and more she was conformed to Christ, and gathering upon her own head, as the guilty one, the sins of all men, she longed to offer herself up — her fragile body now held erect only by an interior flame. She no longer took even a morsel of food or a drop of water: she lived only on the Eucharistic Host, just as her soul lived only upon Christ.

NOTES: *Chapter 31*

1. Latium was an ancient country southeast of Rome. The name is still applied to the region.
2. A hill and public park in Rome; not one of the seven hills.
3. Built A.D. 130 by the Emperor Hadrian as his tomb; turned into a fortress by Honorius (A.D. 423).

## 32. Passing

"I am dying and yet I cannot die, seeing our Creator so grievously offended in the Mystical Body of holy Church, and our Faith contaminated by those who should be keeping it bright," thus, writing to the Milanese Carthusian, Don Pietro, she laid bare the wound from which Christendom was suffering. "I tell you, my dearest father, that whether we wish it or not the times invite us to die," she repeated later on.

And she went each day along the Via di Papa (now Via Santa Chiara) where she was then living, to the basilica of St. Peter, where she assisted at Mass and received Holy Communion. Numerous pilgrimages there reflected her own love which, forgetful of self, rose to the Pope, to the Church, to lose itself in God. One day — Sexagesima Sunday, at the hour of Vespers — as her companions watched her rapt in prayer, repeating her offering to her Spouse, she suddenly collapsed upon the marble floor, as if crushed by a heavy weight. Her tunic was torn; her body writhed on the pavement. Jesus had appeared to her and seemed to place upon those slender shoulders the whole weight of the church nave, that nave of which Giotto had reproduced the mosaic model in the portico of the basilica, to be seen by all who entered the church. It was a collapse from which she never recovered. The next evening, January 30, she broke down again in her room, after dictating to Barduccio a letter to the Pope. It seemed that she was overwhelmed by heavy clouds, plunged into a dark night, in which demons assailed her, furious because she kept them from tearing the Church to pieces. Painfully and with difficulty she raised herself from the floor, with the idea of going to the chapel; in her great weakness she leaned upon Barduccio. However, she had to lie down upon her cot, and it seemed that her soul, escaped from her body, stood apart, looking down upon her corpse. Then her soul, thus free, supplicated her Spouse for the Church, for her followers, for her own salvation; and her Spouse comforted her. Then for two days and nights in succession she was assailed by terrible depression.

In this period of agony Catherine prayed: "To Thee, Eternal Father, I, miserable one, again offer my life for Thy sweet spouse, the Church." She prayed for its reform; she prayed for her disciples, that in case of her death they should not remain orphans but be comforted by the Father with His grace and be made "to live as if dead in true and most perfect life," bound to each other by charity and dying "deeply in love with that sweet spouse," the Church which existed only for them; she prayed that none of them would ever be unfaithful; and she concluded this prayer by deploring her own sins: "I have sinned; have mercy upon me!"

Her physical condition now deteriorated rapidly. One morning during Lent, after Mass and Holy Communion, she was so weak that she had to be carried to her bed. Nevertheless after an hour or two she forced herself to rise and, half alive, she dragged herself to St. Peter's, where she remained in prayer until evening. And thus — as she herself confessed to Fra Raimondo in a long letter dated February 15 — "my life flows out into this sweet spouse, I in my miserable way and the glorious martyrs by their blood."

In that letter she recapitulated to her spiritual father and son the teachings she had imparted through the years and entrusted her writings to his care, among them the *Dialogue*, so that, along with Fra Bartolomeo Dominici, Fra Tommaso della Fonte, maestro Giovanni Tantucci, and Sir Tommaso Buonconti, he might decide the best use to be made of them for the honor of God; finally she commended to him the family of her followers, so that he, as their father and head, might preserve them in charity and humility. She ended by asking his pardon and his blessing. The letter reads like a last will and testament, pervaded by a sweet sorrow in which one senses the nearness of death.

Nevertheless on the following day she dictated another letter to the same Fra Raimondo, in which she urged faith in the Church, declaring herself to be its daughter, its servant, and its soldier, convinced that only through the Church one goes to God and that the duty of the Christian is to enter the field of battle, like a knight, for her, with the shield of holy Faith.

The following night, February 26, the third Sunday of Lent, she became so weak that she could no longer leave her bed; and thus she remained for eight weeks of suffering. The lower part of her body was almost lifeless; only her countenance remained normal.

"And when the sweet time of death will come . . ." she had once said. Now it was at hand. She was undergoing torment in her body and the last trial of her soul: but for Catherine it was sweet to suffer. Visited by God, tortured by the devil, her soul continued to blaze within her frail body, bound to her pallet, in her tiny room transformed into an oratory.

One day all of her disciples present in Rome gathered in that oratory where she offered herself as a holocaust to Christ. Even Stefano Maconi was there, having escaped the tentacles of his family, spurred on by a divine presentiment. One of her followers, the papal protonotary, Tommaso di Petra, in the name of all present, now convinced that death was imminent, begged her to leave them a sort of spiritual testament. She consented, and dictated her last wishes, to which she added, with remarkable clarity of mind, and her customary straightforwardness and simplicity, a recapitulation of her life's teaching, the way of her ascent to God.

To a letter written by Barduccio, to the Benedictine nuns near Florence we owe the account of her death, and these "last words"

pronounced by "the blessed and most happy virgin, Catherine."
The account sets forth the essential features of the asceticism Catherine constantly practiced. She had begun by stripping her heart
of every sensitive love and every created thing, so as to leave it
free, to give it entirely to God, that God sought and desired "through
the path of sufferings." From His hands she had unhesitatingly accepted whatever had happened from day to day, in joys and tribulations; and she had never violated one of His commandments. Illumined by Him, to arrive at perfection she had used the means
of prayer that was humble, faithful, and continuous; this she recommended to her followers. She added the monition never to think
evil of one's neighbor (and upon this point — later on — she was to
give testimony of herself, declaring that never under pretext of any
murmuring or detraction or calumny or injury directed against her,
had she judged evil of them who were responsible, but had always
thought that those who had thus acted or spoken had done so out
of charity and of zeal for her soul: and furthermore such attitude
had saved her "from dangerous judgment of my fellow man."

She pointed out that divine Providence had never failed her and
certainly would not fail them would they but trust in God.

Then, becoming more animated, she made her own the testament of Jesus and she repeated it to them, with insistence: "Love
one another, my children, love one another; for in this way you will
show that you have had me and want me as your mother. And I
shall hold that you are my dearest children so that, being virtuous,
you shall be my glory and my crown. And I shall pray the divine
Goodness that the abundance of all graces and gifts which it has
pleased Him to infuse into my soul, He will cause to overflow into
all of you."

She commended to them the work of reform in the Church and
allegiance to the papacy, to which from the age of seven she had
dedicated the powers of her soul and the torments of her body.
Then clearly and distinctly she said to them: "Be sure of this,
my sweet children, that leaving my body, I shall have in truth consumed my life in the Church and given it for the Church; this is
for me a most particular grace."

Listening to her, one by one her disciples began to weep bitterly. She comforted them, pointing out the advantage of her ascent to her Spouse, yet remaining up to the last, on this point also, completely at the disposal of God's will.

As she sighed in the troubled silence of the little room, and the end seemed imminent, she made them come close to her, one by one, and to each she gave a final word of counsel, that, according to the nature and aptitude of each, all might become holy. Maconi she ordered to enter the Carthusians; Malavolti was to retire to Mt. Olivet; Neri, to become a hermit; the notary, Cristofano, to embrace the religious life in the Siena hospital, as a lay brother; others, to become priests. She named Sister Alessia as superior of her nuns; Fra Raimondo would be superior of the friars, her followers, and, in his absence, Fra William Flete and Matteo di Fazio, the rector of the Pia Casa di Misericordia — a religious and a layman.

Each one accepted, as coming from God, the obedience assigned him; and while she asked pardon of all, they knelt to receive, for the last time, her blessing.

On the evening of Holy Saturday, March 24, summoned by a letter from Catherine, the trusted Bartolomeo Dominici, arrived, to see his spiritual mother stretched out upon a bare pallet, rimmed with a wooden border, like a bier; she seemed, even though wasted away, to be ruddy in complexion, as if tanned by the sun. He bent over her and heard her confession, made in little gasps. Then she said: "I am going now . . . thanks be to our Saviour!"

Nevertheless the following day, Easter Sunday, her thirty-third birthday, she rose from her bed to assist at Mass and receive Holy Communion from the celebrant, Fra Bartolomeo. Every moment seemed to bring her nearer to her divine Spouse; although her body was a mere skeleton, her face shone like an angel's. The presence of Fra Bartolomeo was a comfort to her in her last hours, yet she told him to leave her and assist Fra Raimondo, whose election as Master General of the Dominicans was imminent.

During the night of April 29, the Sunday before the feast of the Ascension, the crisis came and her disciples, aroused from sleep, gathered around her bed. With a nod, she asked again for absolution, and then received Extreme Unction. After receiving the last sacraments, she seemed stricken with interior agitation which spasmodically expressed itself on her face and in the movement of her arms: the last battle with the spirits of darkness. And she commenced to whisper sadly: "I have sinned, O Lord; have mercy upon me!" repeating this invocation many times, each time raising her right arm and then letting it fall of its own weight.

Then she was calmer, and began to repeat: "Holy God, have mercy upon me!" The horrors of sin had diminished. Her troubled countenance again became calm and her eyes, which had been clouded and filled with tears, were now bright with serene joy, so that those around her were comforted.

Sister Alessia held Catherine's head to her breast and, at the request of the dying woman, with the help of those present, had her sit up upon the bed, holding her in her arms. For those present she was their dearest mother; for Rome, she was a part of that city "where Christ is Roman"; for Italy, she was the peacemaker; for Christendom, she was one of its greatest creatures, to take her place alongside of a Paul, an Augustine, a Bernard, a Francis, a Dominic.

With her gaze fixed upon the crucifix, she remained long in contemplation and adoration. She accused herself again of ignorance, of ingratitude, of disobedience, whether in striving for the honor of God or in serving souls in forming her community "in singular love." Again she asked for absolution; again she adored the crucifix; again she gave words of counsel to her children; again she asked the blessings of her mother, Lapa, who, along with other disciples, wept.

Still praying, she whispered: "Thou, O Lord, callest me and I am coming to Thee; and I come not through my own merits but only through Thy mercy."

Again she prayed for the Church and for Pope Urban VI whom she proclaimed to be the true Pope and Vicar of Christ upon earth. Then she repeated for her disciples the words of blessing pronounced by Christ at the Last Supper: "Thine they were, and to me thou hast entrusted them. . . . Keep them loyal to thy name . . . that none of them be lost" (Jn. 17:6, 11, 12).

She blessed them again, one by one, and also gave a blessing for those absent.

Few creatures have ever longed for death with such pure love. For Catherine this earthly life was a struggle to free herself from the bonds of the devil, the world, and the flesh, by the light of reason and the forces of faith; to be redeemed, freed, to become Christ. She freed herself from her own will to become the will of God. She was immersed in the Blood of Christ, the price of this freedom.

Now breaking the last bit of that bond she cried: "Blood, Blood!" The time was noon, April 29, a Sunday. She was thirty-three years old, as was Christ upon the cross. Like Christ, she made a last invocation: "Father, into Thy hands I commend my spirit!" With these words she died.